W9-CPP-621

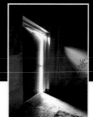

The Mysterious & Unknown

The Kennedy Assassination

by David Robson

ReferencePoint Press™

San Diego, CA

For more information, contact:
ReferencePoint Press, Inc.
PO Box 27779
San Diego, CA 92198
www.ReferencePointPress.com

Picture credits:
cover: AP Images
AP Images: 6, 10, 12, 13, 15, 16, 19, 23, 24, 27, 30, 31, 32, 36, 39, 42, 45, 48, 53, 64, 69, 78
Landov: 34
Tony Strom: 52, 81

Series design and book layout: Amy Stirnkorb

LIBRARY OF CONGRESS CATALOGING-IN-PUBLICATION DATA

Robson, David.
  Kennedy assassination / by David Robson.
    p. cm. -- (The mysterious & unknown series)
Includes bibliographical references and index.
ISBN-13: 978-1-60152-036-4 (hardback)
ISBN-10: 1-60152-036-0 (hardback)

1. Kennedy, John F. (John Fitzgerald), 1917–1963--Assassination. I. Title.
E842.9.R578 2008
364.152'4--dc22

2007035064

CONTENTS

FOREWORD

> "Strange is our situation here upon earth."
> —*Albert Einstein*

Since the beginning of recorded history, people have been perplexed, fascinated, and even terrified by events that defy explanation. While science has demystified many of these events, such as volcanic eruptions and lunar eclipses, some continue to remain outside the scope of the provable. Do UFOs exist? Are people abducted by aliens? Can some people see into the future? These questions and many more continue to puzzle, intrigue, and confound despite the enormous advances of modern science and technology.

It is these questions, phenomena, and oddities that Reference-Point Press's *The Mysterious & Unknown* series is committed to exploring. Each volume examines historical and anecdotal evidence as well as the most recent theories surrounding the topic in debate. Fascinating primary source quotes from scientists, experts, and eyewitnesses, as well as in-depth sidebars further inform the text. Full-color illustrations and photos add to each book's visual appeal. Finally, source notes, a bibliography, and a thorough index provide further reference and research support. Whether for research or the curious reader, *The Mysterious & Unknown* series is certain to satisfy those fascinated by the unexplained.

INTRODUCTION

"Death in the Family"

Twelve-year-old Eric Jones sat in English class waiting for the bell to ring. It was Friday, November 22, 1963, and the seventh grader was looking forward to the day's scheduled assembly.

Suddenly, the principal's voice came over the loudspeaker: "May I have your attention!" Rarely did the principal interrupt class time. A hush fell over the room. "In Dallas, Texas, today, President Kennedy was shot,"[1] he said. Students and teachers gasped.

Like many other Americans that day, Eric Jones was sure the president would be all right. John F. Kennedy was, after all, the most powerful man in the world. He was charming, good looking, and full of life. Eric identified with the president's children, too, only a few years younger than he was. The boy felt, as many Americans did, like he knew the Kennedy family.

It was not until later that day, when school let out, that Eric

President John F. Kennedy was assassinated on November 22, 1963.

learned what the rest of the world already knew. Kennedy was dead, killed by a sniper's bullet. "It was worse than 9/11," Jones says now, referring to the terrorist attacks of September 11, 2001. "It was like a death in the family."[2] Many Americans who were alive at the time have similar memories of the Kennedy assassination. They knew this man—at least they felt like they did. For four days—from assassination to funeral—the nation was paralyzed with shock and grief.

Kennedy was the fourth president of the United States to be assassinated while in office. The first, Abraham Lincoln, was shot in a Washington, D.C., theater in 1865, only days after the end of the Civil War. Lincoln, like Kennedy, had led the country through a time of great peril.

James Garfield, murdered by religious fanatic Charles Guiteau in 1881, had spent only 6 months in office and was little known by the general public. William McKinley was shot in 1901 by

Through a Glass, Darkly

Abraham Zapruder was a staunch supporter of the Democratic Party and of Kennedy in particular. He immigrated to the United States in 1920 from Ukraine. In the early 1940s he started a clothing company—Nardis—with a partner. Two decades later he had his own business. He ran it in a building adjacent to the Texas School Book Depository in Dallas.

On November 22 Zapruder left home without his Bell & Howell movie camera. When he got to work his secretary told him to go home and get his camera so he could record the motorcade. After the shooting, Zapruder made three copies of the film, keeping the original. Eventually, he sold the original and the rights to the film to *Life* magazine for $150,000. He donated part of the proceeds from the sale to the family of Officer J.D. Tippit, killed in the line of duty that day.

anarchist Leon F. Czolgosz, who saw the president as an enemy of the working people. McKinley's vice president, Theodore Roosevelt, became the youngest man ever to hold the office at the age of 43.

Kennedy's sudden death, unlike the others', occurred in the mid-twentieth century, an era dominated by a new medium: television. Not only were journalists able to report the latest on the president's condition, but they could interview witnesses at the scene; speak to federal officials and police officers; and carry events, such as the president's funeral, live for millions to see and experience. In the late fall of 1963 the country's collective grief was shared from coast to coast.

But that was not all. In the hours after Kennedy's fateful ride through the streets of Dallas, a startling revelation was made: The assassination had been caught on film. Local dressmaker Abraham Zapruder was standing on a concrete street divider as Kennedy's car passed. His 8-millimeter Bell & Howell camera caught the assassination in all of its gory detail. In time, the 21-second Zapruder film not only became the most watched home movie ever made but a crucial piece of evidence in the hunt for the president's killer.

Researchers who surf the Internet today, decades later, will find dozens of Web sites dedicated to the Kennedy assassination. Americans, it seems, are not satisfied with the official version of this tragic event. Instead, professional and amateur sleuths spend countless hours hunting for new clues and novel ways of looking at the old ones. For them it is an obsession. The most investigated crime in history continues to haunt new generations because the murder of a president, by one man or as the product of a conspiracy, demands a resolution.

CHAPTER 1

"Why Worry About It?"

November 22, 1963, dawned dark and cloudy. Despite the ominous weather, Texans tried to make the best of things. It was a rare occasion, after all, when John Fitzgerald Kennedy, the nation's thirty-fifth president, visited the Lone Star State.

The general excitement was not unanimous, though. In the 1960 presidential election, Kennedy won a slim victory in Texas. His vice president, a long, tall, 55-year-old Texan named Lyndon Baines Johnson, had been added to the Kennedy ticket primarily to secure a Democratic victory in the South, and the two men were not exactly close friends.

Once elected, Kennedy's attempts to negotiate peace with the Soviet Union—Cold War enemy of the United States—and his support for civil rights particularly, made him politically vulnerable in Dixie. For many in the South, Kennedy—the youngest man

In 1962 racial tensions bubbled up when black college student James Meredith was denied admission to the University of Mississippi. The governor, Ross Barnet, personally assumed the position of registrar and blocked Meredith from enrollment.

ever elected to the nation's highest office—was an Irish-Catholic Yankee who did not mind his own business. His dashing smile and perfect hair were a mark of arrogance, they thought. He did not understand their way of life.

At the time, racism against African Americans was rampant in the South, and civil rights was a touchy issue. The landmark Supreme Court case *Brown v. Board of Education*, which ended racial segregation in public schools, was less than 10 years old. In 1962 racial tensions bubbled up again when black college student James Meredith was denied admission to the University of Mississippi. Southern liberal and conservative Democrats were feuding, as they disagreed about the direction of their party. Now Kennedy had come, in large part, to mend political fences and guarantee that Texas stayed in the Democratic column in the 1964 presidential election.

Regardless of the political reasons for the visit, Texas was a risky place for a liberal Democrat like Kennedy. Some local journalists and many citizens even questioned the president's judgment in making the trip. The front-page headline of the *Dallas Morning News* that day said it all: "Storm of Political Controversy Swirls Around Kennedy on Visit."[3] Kennedy was an unpopular president in the South, and recent Dallas political history merely echoed the feeling.

Less than a month earlier, ambassador to the United Nations Adlai Stevenson was hit with a protestor's sign and spit on after giving a speech at Dallas's Memorial Auditorium Theater. Johnson and his wife were shouted at and jeered during the campaign of 1960. "We were a little worried when we left for Texas," said CBS News correspondent Robert Pierpoint. "The general atmosphere was very anti-Kennedy, so we were concerned even before we left that there might be some incidents."[4]

For these reasons, close friend Senator William Fulbright warned Kennedy, "Dallas is a very dangerous place."[5] In spite of the ominous portents, Kennedy was determined to make the trip. He was even fatalistic about the dangers.

On the morning of November 22, the *Dallas Morning News* ran an ad from the conservative John Birch Society suggesting that Kennedy and his brother Robert, the attorney general, were pro-Communist. Showing the ad to his wife Jacqueline, the president simply said, "If somebody wants to shoot me from a window with a rifle, nobody can stop it, so why worry about it?"[6]

Landing at Love Field

The warnings notwithstanding, Kennedy was feeling confident. He had a secret weapon in his public relations arsenal: the First

President Kennedy and his wife, Jacqueline, arrive at Love Field in Dallas, on the morning of November 22, 1963. Shortly after their arrival the president would be dead.

Lady of the United States. Jacqueline Bouvier Kennedy, a dark-haired beauty admired for her style and decorum, was making her first domestic political trip with her husband.

The head of state and his glamorous spouse were the closest thing the country had to royalty. Both had come from privileged backgrounds, and widely published photos of the couple and their two children—Caroline and John Jr. (John-John)—presented a picture of youth and vigor that captured the public's imagination. One newsman announced Kennedy's arrival in Dallas by joking, "I can see his suntan all the way from here."[7]

The president recognized that his soft-spoken wife was far more popular with the masses than he was. At 8:45 that morning,

Kennedy left Forth Worth's Texas Hotel, where he had stayed the night before. He walked across the street to speak with a crowd gathered in a parking lot. They were disappointed his wife was not with him, and Kennedy joked about her absence. "Mrs. Kennedy is organizing herself," he told the people. "It takes longer, but, of course, she looks better than we do when she does it."[8]

During their two-day stay in Texas, the president and First Lady were escorted by Texas governor John Connally and his wife, Nellie. When the four landed at Love Field in Dallas at

This image, taken moments before Kennedy's assassination, shows the Kennedys in the limo with Texas governor John Connally and his wife, Nellie.

11:38 a.m., after the short flight from Fort Worth, Mrs. Connally noticed that the gloom of the day had lifted. "Even the clouds themselves miraculously parted and drenched the scene in sunlight," she said years later. "We were sure the rest of the day would go as well."[9]

Jacqueline then John Kennedy appeared at the door of the plane. The First Lady—wearing a raspberry-colored suit and matching pillbox hat—was greeted with a bouquet of red roses. "The first impression of her stepping to the door will linger forever," says Mike Quinn, reporter for the *Dallas Morning News.* "The crowd seemed awestruck, then started applauding and— if you will pardon—squealing. I understood then why Kennedy liked to have Mrs. Kennedy along."[10] The president, meanwhile, conversed with well-wishers, shaking outstretched hands and waving.

After these few moments at the airport, Governor and Mrs. Connally joined President and Mrs. Kennedy in the black Ford limousine that would carry them to a noontime luncheon in central Dallas. The president asked aides about the weather and when he heard the report decided to keep the removable top off the car.

According to political writer Jack Bell, the Secret Service wanted to drive the Kennedys directly to the Trade Mart, where the president would be giving a speech. But Johnson had convinced the president otherwise. "He wanted Kennedy to go through Dallas," says Bell, "and demonstrate to these people— and to the world—that Dallas loved Kennedy."[11]

The plan was for the president's motorcade to slowly drive the 10 miles (16km) or so from Love Field, passing the thousands of waving Texans that had lined the route. While many held plac-

"You certainly cannot say that Dallas doesn't love you."

—Nellie Connally, wife of the Texas governor, says to President Kennedy moments before shots ring out.

ards of support like "Onward J.F.K.," others were less welcoming. One read "Let's Bury King John."[12]

Ride Through Dallas

Clint Hill, a 32-year-old Secret Service agent, was one of the men charged with protecting the president that day. For Hill, this meant sitting on the fender of the car directly behind the Kennedys and scanning the throngs of people from behind dark sunglasses.

So far, though, it seemed Hill had little to worry about. All was going according to plan, and as the motorcade began, Nellie Connally was very pleased. "I felt tingly all over," she said later, "with the pride of a mother whose children are performing just as I had hoped."[13] The two couples talked back and forth when they could—the Kennedys in the back seat and a little higher, the Connallys in the front near the driver—but it was hard to hear over the din of the cheering spectators.

Reporters covering the day in Dallas were not having as much fun. Crammed into press buses and stuck behind the motorcade, most of them viewed the presidential parade as routine. "I was behind the driver," said *Time* correspondent Hugh Sidey, "and to be honest I was bored. It was just another motorcade."[14] For journalists like Sidey, the real story would begin with the president's remarks at the Trade Mart.

The motorcade was in the heart of the city now. The crowd swelled and roared its approval. The president and First Lady smiled and waved from the open car like Hollywood stars at a movie premiere. "Kennedy had this marvelous— it wasn't a wave, it was an acknowledgement with his hand up,"[15] says Pierce Allman, program manager at WFAA-TV. All had

Special Agent Clint Hill, a 32-year-old Secret Service agent, was one of the men charged with protecting the president that day. For Hill, this meant sitting on the fender of the car directly behind the Kennedys and scanning the throngs of people from behind dark sunglasses.

Seconds
after the
president was
shot, Agent
Hill sprang
into action
by jumping
on the mov-
ing limo and
covering the
president
with his body
to shield him
from further
harm.

gone better than planned. Despite political divisions, citizens of Dallas had come out to give the president a big Texas welcome.

At about 12:30 the limousine approached Dealey Plaza and prepared to pass beneath the triple underpass of Commerce, Elm, and Main Streets. Nellie Connally spoke over her shoulder: "Mr. President," she said, "you certainly cannot say that Dallas doesn't love you."[16]

"They Are Going to Kill Us All"

Kennedy smiled at the compliment, and then came a sound— like an exploding firecracker. The president's face went blank. He clutched his throat—elbows in the air—and sunk into his seat. Instantly, Governor Connally was hit in the chest. "My God, they are going to kill us all,"[17] he screamed.

At the first sound of gunfire, Hill scrambled toward the limousines as the two women desperately tried pulling their husbands from the line of fire. President Kennedy wore a stiff brace from years of back pain and was not easy to move.

Another shot rang out. It shattered the right side of the president's skull, spraying blood and pieces of brain across the car seats. Mrs. Kennedy, in a frantic attempt to retrieve the back of her husband's head, climbed toward the rear of the car.

Just at that moment, Hill reached the panicked First Lady. He pushed her back into the limousine and did what he could to shield her and the mortally wounded president.

Abraham Zapruder, perched above the scene, lowered his camera, stunned. He had watched the president pass before his lens, and what he had seen horrified him. He collected his thoughts and rushed from Dealey Plaza, camera in hand.

When he arrived at WFAA-TV in Dallas, Zapruder described what he saw to a reporter. It was one of the first eyewitness accounts of the shooting:

> ZAPRUDER: As the President's coming down from Houston Street, making his turn, it was about half-way down there, I heard a shot and he slumped to the side, like this. Then I heard another shot or two. I couldn't tell you whether it was one or two. And I saw his head practically open up, all blood and everything. And I kept on shooting. That's about all. I'm just sick. I can't—
> REPORTER: I think that pretty well expresses the entire feelings of the whole world.
> ZAPRUDER: Terrible. [18]

Rush to the Hospital

After the shooting, the president's car immediately broke from the motorcade and picked up speed. Within moments the limousine arrived at Parkland Hospital. Mrs. Kennedy held her husband in her arms and cried.

> "I'm not going to let him go," she told Agent Clint Hill.
> "We've got to take him in, Mrs. Kennedy," he said.
> "No, Mr. Hill," she said. "You know he's dead. Let me alone."
> After Hill handed her his jacket to wrap around the president's head, the First Lady cried out, "He's dead—they've killed him—Oh Jack, oh Jack, I love you."[19]

Despite Mrs. Kennedy's pained protests, the president and Connally were rushed into the hospital on stretchers. And before long a confused press corps arrived, asking questions and trying to nail down the extent of the president's injuries.

By now, dignitaries at the Trade Mart had been told that something had gone horribly wrong. The speech they would never hear Kennedy give spoke of understanding and reliance on common sense to overcome political differences. According to the text of the prepared speech he planned to give: "We cannot expect that everyone will 'talk sense to the American people.' But we can hope that fewer people will listen to nonsense."[20] Now, all sense was gone, and understanding was overwhelmed by unspeakable tragedy.

The real story, though, was inside the operating rooms at Parkland Hospital, and very little information was leaking out. Early news reports said only that the president and governor had been shot. Reporters worked their sources to get the latest and most accurate medical information.

What the reporters did not know until afterward was that Kennedy was operated on for 40 minutes. At one point, eight doctors tended to him. Later, attending surgeon Malcolm Perry provided his initial impression. "It was apparent that the president had sustained a lethal wound," he said. "A missile had gone in and out of the back of his head."[21] But few at the time were aware of this dark prognosis. Instead, the world was watching and waiting, hoping for some good news.

Malcolm Kilduff, assistant White House press secretary, made the devastating announcement that the president was killed about an hour after the incident.

It never came. Barely an hour after the shooting Malcolm Kilduff, assistant White House press secretary, made the devastating announcement to the press. "President John F. Kennedy died at approximately 1 o'clock Central Standard Time today here in Dallas. He died of a gunshot wound to the brain."[22] Connally, said Kilduff, was in "serious" but not "critical" condition.

CBS News anchor Walter Cronkite, broadcasting to an anxious nation, was handed Kilduff's statement. Cronkite put on his glasses, read it, removed his glasses, looked into the camera, and

Kennedy is one of
two presidents buried
at Arlington National
Cemetery. The other is
William Howard Taft.
The twenty-seventh
president also served
as chief justice of
the United States for
a time.

broke the dreadful news. His voiced cracked as he spoke. "From Dallas, Texas, the flash, apparently official: President Kennedy died at 1:00 P.M., Central Standard Time, two o'clock, Eastern Standard Time—some thirty-eight minutes ago."[23]

More details soon emerged. Perry and Kemp Clark, chief of neurosurgery, reported that the president was hit by a bullet in the throat, just below the Adam's apple. The men agreed that this looked like an entry wound. Kennedy also had a wound in his back and a massive one on the right side of his head. They could not tell whether two or three bullets had pierced the president's body.

The doctors added one more important detail—one that, like the entry wound description, remains in dispute. In a desperate attempt to revive Kennedy, the medical team performed a tracheotomy, a technique in which a small hole is cut in the throat to help the patient's breathing. Investigators would later wonder whether this procedure destroyed evidence that would definitively determine whether Kennedy's front throat wound was one of entry or exit.

Chief surgeon at Parkland Hospital Tom Shires issued a statement that night. "Medically, it was apparent the president was not alive when he was brought in," he said. "I am absolutely sure he never knew what hit him."[24]

"All I Can Do"

At 2:00 P.M. Kennedy's bronze coffin was carried from Parkland Hospital. Jacqueline Kennedy, the widowed First Lady, walked beside it, her eyes cast downward. She had removed her pillbox hat, and when her husband's casket was placed in an ambulance for the somber ride to Love Field, she climbed in after it.

Brain Matters

One of the central pieces of evidence in the assassination of John F. Kennedy was the president's brain. When Kennedy's lifeless body was wheeled into the operating room, doctors could immediately see that massive head trauma had occurred, but to confirm where the fatal shot came from they would have to examine the brain more closely. They never got that chance. In the weeks and months after the assassination, Attorney General Robert Kennedy took control of all of the physical materials related to his brother's death. Although the circumstances surrounding Robert Kennedy's involvement are murky, one thing is quite probable: While the president's body was interred at Arlington National Cemetery in 1963, Kennedy's brain resides, to this day, in a separate location. In 1978, after a thorough investigation, the House Select Committee concluded it was likely that Robert Kennedy either destroyed the materials—including the brain—or put them out of the public's reach in an attempt to squelch further questions.

Air Force One, the presidential jet, was heavily guarded and parked on a private runway. The ambulance arrived, and the president's casket was loaded onto the plane.

Fearing another assassination attempt, Johnson insisted he be sworn in while still in Dallas. Local judge Sarah Hughes was summoned to the airport to administer the oath of office. A few members of the press were also allowed aboard Air Force One to witness the momentous occasion. United Press International reporter Merriman Smith described the transfer of power:

> All of the shades of the larger main cabin were drawn. The interior was hot and dimly lit. There were twenty-seven people in the compartment. Johnson stood in the center with his wife, Lady Bird. The compartment became hotter and hotter. It developed that Johnson was waiting for Mrs. Kennedy, who was composing herself in a small bedroom in the rear of the plane. She appeared alone, dressed in the same pink suit she had worn in the morning when she appeared so happy shaking hands with airport crowds at the side of her husband. She was white-faced but dry-eyed.[25]

Mrs. Kennedy's blood-spattered stockings were a brutal testament to the day's shocking truth. She refused to change her clothes, she said, because she wanted the people of Dallas to see what they had done.

Johnson asked someone for a glass of water, gulped it down, and, when prompted by Hughes, raised his right hand and placed his left on the Bible. "I do solemnly swear," Johnson said, "I will faithfully execute the office of president of the United States."

Jacqueline Kennedy gets into the ambulance carrying her husband's body. Her dress and legs are still covered in the blood of her late husband.

With that, Johnson turned to his wife, Lady Bird, and offered a kiss. He turned to Mrs. Kennedy and consoled her. The hasty ceremony—the first under such dire circumstances—was over. Eight minutes later, Air Force One was in the air and headed home. "It was really the most amazing thing," said a witness, reporter Sid Davis:

Lyndon B. Johnson was sworn in as president on Air Force One on the same day Kennedy was shot. Jacqueline Kennedy stood at his side, still stunned from the day's events.

What you had was the new president of the United States on the airplane, the body of the fallen president in a casket in the back of the airplane, the widow of the fallen president, and the wife of the new president on this plane going back to Washington. It said something about the strength of this country, the fact that we had this thing happen, we didn't know who did it or why they did it, but the transition from one man to another was done in an orderly way.[26]

As the new president's plane flew back to the nation's capital, words of condolence and even anger were pouring in. French president Charles de Gaulle said that Kennedy had "died like a soldier, under fire for his duty and in the service of his country."[27]

Former American president Dwight D. Eisenhower, the retired general Kennedy had replaced, was indignant. "I share the sense of shock and dismay that the entire nation must feel," he told the press, "at the despicable act that took the life of the nation's president."[28] One veteran senator from Montana called the murder a "mark upon the responsibility and respectability of some of our citizens."[29]

At 6:00 P.M., under cover of darkness, Air Force One landed at Andrews Air Force Base in Maryland. The president's dark brown coffin was lowered from the plane by a lift truck. Secret Service agents then placed the casket into the arms of an honor guard who moved it to a navy ambulance. Jacqueline Kennedy and her brother-in-law Robert Kennedy held hands and followed the president's body into the waiting car.

A few moments later President Lyndon Baines Johnson stepped to a horde of microphones to utter his first words as commander in chief. The plane's engine roared behind him; the new First Lady stood to his left, clutching her purse. "I will do my best," he told a grieving nation. "That is all I can do. I ask for your help—and God's"[30]

CHAPTER 2

Hunt for a Killer

With President Kennedy dead, slain in broad daylight, attention focused on the scene of the crime. Immediately after the shots rang out at Dealey Plaza, Dallas police swarmed the area. Several onlookers swore the shots had come from above and behind the president's limousine—specifically from the Texas School Book Depository, a red brick building less than 100 yards (91m) from the site of the assassination.

One eyewitness, TV reporter Mel Crouch, told investigators that at the first shot he saw a rifle peeking and then disappearing from the "fifth or six floor"[31] of the depository. Gayle and William Newman—standing 15 feet (4.5m) in front of the president's car—dropped to the ground and shielded their small children when they heard the shots. Unlike Crouch, the Newmans were

certain the gunfire had come from a nearby patch of lawn known as the grassy knoll, not the book depository. Another witness, Lee Bowers, had no doubt he had seen a flash of light coming from a railroad tower behind the knoll.

Other people had other stories. Amid the chaos, two eyewitnesses were taken into custody by the police for further questioning. The one thing on which all could agree was that in the immediate aftermath of the assassination confusion and fear spread through the stunned crowd. Dallas police could only desperately clutch at the dozens of leads they were receiving and hope to find a suspect or suspects.

Strangely, a second crime committed less than an hour after the assassination drew police closer to a possible culprit. As the massive manhunt for the killer ensued, police headquarters received an anonymous report of a policeman being shot.

The Texas School Book Depository, left, is where the shooter is said to have been perched waiting to shoot the president.

Officer J.D. Tippit, who had heard reports of the assassination and was on the lookout for a white male, 5' 10" (1.78m), 165 pounds (74.8kg), was patrolling Tenth Street near the intersection with Patton Avenue in the Oak Cliff section of town. At 1:14 P.M., Tippit noticed a man fitting the suspect's general description walking along the sidewalk and called the man over to his patrol car for a chat.

Neighborhood witnesses observed what appeared to be a friendly conversation between the 2 men. Then suddenly, all talk came to an abrupt halt when Tippit got out of his car and walked toward the left front fender. Without warning, the mystery man drew a .38-caliber pistol and fired 3 to 4 times at Tippit, who fell to the ground. The gunman then approached Tippit and fired once at point-blank range into his head.

"This Is It!"

Less than an hour later, police received a call from the Texas Theatre, a movie house located at 231 West Jefferson Boulevard. An usher had alerted cashier Julie Postal about a customer acting oddly inside. Another version of the story says that Postal called the police for help when the customer entered without paying for a ticket. The two features listed on the marquee that day were *Cry of Battle* and *War Is Hell*. When Postal made the fateful call she could not know that the sleepy theater would soon host its own primal struggle. The Texas Theatre was located six blocks from the site of Tippit's murder.

In a matter of moments, a squad of police cars—their sirens blaring—arrived on the scene. At least a dozen policemen entered the darkened theater and began searching patrons, starting at the front of the house. A shoe store clerk, who had seen the mystery man enter, pointed him out to Officer N.M. McDonald, and as McDonald approached, the small, scruffy man jumped out of his seat. "This is it!"[32] the man shouted. McDonald drew his gun and was greeted with the man's own .38-caliber pistol. The two scuffled and fell over the seats. A group of officers rushed to McDonald's aid and subdued the suspect, but not before he pulled the trigger of his gun. It misfired.

The suspect was arrested on the spot for the murder of J.D. Tippit. As police dragged him from the theater, he shouted, "I know my rights. I want a lawyer."[33] He needed one. Once in custody, he would initially be charged in the death of a police officer. Before long, though, eyewitness testimony and key pieces of evidence would place him at the scene of another crime: the assassination of the president.

On the drive to police headquarters, the suspect remained calm and collected, divulging little. He refused to tell the arresting officers his name or where he lived. "I know my rights," he told them again. Still, he did not look surprised when told of the charges against him. He angered police with his smart-aleck responses, as described by author Gerald Posner:

> "Police officer been killed?" he asked. It was silent for a moment, and then he said, "I hear they burn for murder," referring to the death penalty given to convicted killers. Officer C.T. Walker, sitting on the suspect's right side, tried to control his temper: "You may find out." Again, the suspect smirked. "Well, they say it just takes a second to die," he said.[34]

Oswald was arrested in this Dallas movie theater shortly after the president was shot. Police were alerted regarding a man acting strangely and arrested him immediately.

The mystery man was carrying two identifications, one under the name of Lee Harvey Oswald, the other as A. Hidell. When asked at police headquarters which one he was, he said simply, "You figure it out."[35] Thus, in the absence of the suspect's cooperation, investigators had to verify the man's identity themselves and then piece together his background, all the while searching for clues that would connect him to the Tippit killing. This did not prove easy, but what authorities eventually found startled them.

Misfit

Lee Harvey Oswald was born in 1939 in New Orleans, Louisiana, to a single mother. Oswald and his older brother Robert were often shuffled from place to place, sometimes living with their mother, Marguerite, sometimes staying in orphanages or with distant relatives. These were the years that marked Oswald for the rest of his life.

"You go back to the death of Dad two months before he was born—that's a tremendous impact," says Robert. "What Lee missed from his childhood, in comparison to me, was the whole family being together all the time, the continuity there, the stability."[36]

Young Oswald did not make friends easily, either, and often felt neglected. Author Michael L. Kurtz describes Oswald as a "misfit, unable or unwilling to accommodate himself to the society in which he lived."[37]

In 1952, after Marguerite's third divorce, the family moved to New York City, a vast metropolis in which Oswald, by now a teenager, felt even more lost. He often skipped school and soon found himself in trouble with the law. While in juvenile detention, social workers and at least one psychiatrist studied the boy and concluded he was in need of serious help. In diagnosing a variety of disorders, clinicians determined that Oswald's lack of a father figure made him very capable of violent acts.

Although Marguerite and her sons returned to New Orleans in 1954, it may have been too late to help Oswald, who simply withdrew further into himself. He later recorded his thoughts of himself in a diary. "The son of an insurance salesman whose early death left a far mean streak of independence brought on by neglect."[38]

Bored with school and feeling neglected by his family, Oswald looked for something, anything, to latch on to. "I was looking for a key to my environment," he wrote, "and then I discovered socialist literature."[39] Prompted in part by the execution of convicted American spies Julius and Ethel Rosenberg, Oswald studied Marxism, a political and social movement allied to communism—a movement that frightened many in the 1950s. To pro-

In 1959 Oswald defected to the Soviet Union, a powerful country whose system of government was founded upon the principles of communism. There, Oswald married a Russian named Marina, who would bear him two children. Pictured are Oswald and Marina in Minsk.

fess such beliefs at the time, as he apparently did, was considered not only un-American but treasonous.

At 17, Oswald joined the U.S. Marines Corps and continued to study the controversial philosophies, which did not sit well with his superiors or his fellow soldiers. For this and other reasons, he did not seem cut out to be a military man, as Posner attests:

> Just a year after entering, he wounds himself with a pistol that he's not supposed to have and, as a result, he's court-martialed and then he's put on K.P. (Kitchen Patrol) duty for a very long stint. Eventually, he attacks the sergeant that he believes is responsible for his long Kitchen Patrol service in a bar and challenges him to a fight. Then he's court-martialed a second time. This time he's put into the brig and this has an effect on him. The brig is very hard. And when he comes out, he's now an embittered person.[40]

During his stint in the marines, Oswald also qualified as a sharpshooter on the rifle range, the second highest position possible. More alarming still, at least to Dallas investigators in 1963, was Oswald's 1959 defection to the Soviet Union, a powerful country whose system of government was founded upon the principles of communism. There, Oswald worked in a factory in Minsk and married a Russian named Marina, who would bear him two children.

Oswald biographer Priscilla Johnson McMillan met him in Moscow that first year. He was a rare bird: an American who praised the Soviet system and wanted to live within it. But McMillan saw something deeper than politics at work. "Everything about him spelt loneliness and aloneness," she says now. He left the United States, he told her, because of the things he despised about the American system, "particularly capitalism and racial discrimination."[41]

But even his stay in what he thought would be a Communist paradise was short-lived. After only a few years, "He had become disillusioned with life here," says Russian friend Pavel Golovachev. "He came here after reading a lot of [Karl] Marx and [Vladimir] Lenin, thinking that it was something good. But living here, he realized it was not so good."[42]

Ruth and Marina

Now, almost four years after his military discharge and only months after his Soviet sojourn ended, 24-year-old Oswald returned to the United States. But barely able to survive on his string of menial jobs, Marina and Oswald had to live apart. Marina found a friend and student of Russian in Ruth Paine, an Irving, Texas, housewife who was happy to put her up; Oswald rented a small room in the Oak Cliff section of Dallas, near downtown.

Oswald often visited Marina and the children on weekends, and Paine quickly developed a dislike for him. "I was wanting to get along with this fellow,"[43] she said years later, but Lee made it difficult. Paine often heard him berating Marina in Russian, and the young woman also showed signs of physical abuse.

On October 14, 1963, Paine and Marina shared coffee with Linnie Mae Randle, a neighbor. Oswald had recently lost another job. Randle told them that the Texas School Book Depository, where her brother worked, was hiring. Later that day, Paine called warehouse manager Roy Truly and landed Oswald an interview. "Lee pleased his potential new boss by calling him sir"[44] and got the job.

Oswald, seen here at police headquarters for questioning on November 22, 1963, refused to answer questions or even identify himself when first arrested.

New Job

Oswald worked at the Texas School Book Depository for about six weeks. He often rode to work with coworker Buell Frazier, Randle's brother. According to Randle, at 7:15 A.M. on the morning of Friday, November 22, she was standing at her kitchen sink when she looked out the window and saw Oswald walking across the street with a long package under his arm. After stowing the package in Frazier's car, he approached the window and "stared at Randle until she called out to her brother that he was waiting for his ride."[45] On the way to work, Frazier asked Oswald what was in the package. Curtain rods, Oswald told him.

Later that morning at work, as crowds gathered outside in anticipation of the president's visit, Oswald asked coworker James Jarman what was going on. When Jarman informed him of the coming presidential motorcade, Oswald asked him which direction it would take. Jarman said it would pass directly in front of the book depository.

The sixth floor of the Texas School Book Depository was a warehouse, crammed with heavy boxes. Seven large double windows looked out onto Elm Street and Dealey Plaza. At about 11:40, worker Bonnie Ray Williams noticed Oswald gazing down onto the plaza. Another employee, Charles Givens, was on his way to lunch when he realized he forgot his pack of cigarettes. He hopped back on the elevator and went

to retrieve them. "When I got back upstairs, he was on the sixth floor . . . in that vicinity . . . toward the window up front where the shots were fired from."[46] As far as anyone remembers, Oswald was the only one left up there.

More Charges and a Transfer

Late on the evening of November 22, Dallas police and federal officers charged Oswald with the assassination of Kennedy. In making the announcement, Captain William Fritz held up an Italian-made Mannlicher-Carcano rifle found behind boxes in the Texas School Book Depository.

Fritz also identified Oswald as a member of the Fair Play for Cuba Committee, a leftist organization that supported the rights of Cuba, a Communist country led by revolutionary Fidel Castro. The original complaint against Oswald said that he did, "in furtherance of an international communist conspiracy"[47] murder the president.

That night, though, President Lyndon Johnson ordered the Dallas district attorney to drop any reference to a Communist conspiracy. Although Johnson worried that such a charge might be true, he was also afraid to spark an international crisis.

As for Oswald, he denied the killings of Kennedy and Tippit but then tweaked the nation's suspicions. When confronted by dozens of reporters jammed into the police station and asked directly whether he had shot the president, he replied, "No. I'm just a patsy."[48] Could Oswald, despite the apparently overwhelming evidence against him, simply have been a patsy, a straw man, an assassin supported by some mysterious organization or foreign government?

The answer to that question would have to wait. On Sunday, November 24, after 30 hours of questioning, police decided to

"He came here after reading a lot of Marx and Lenin, thinking that it was something good. Living here, he realized it was not so good."

—Oswald's friend Pavel Golovachev, describing the suspect's disappointment with the Soviet system.

move Oswald from the city jail to the county jail a mile away. An armored van would be used for the short trip to avoid any attempts on the alleged assassin's life.

At 11 A.M. the van was backed into the garage of the municipal building. Oswald was to be led out of a doorway in the building's basement and walked up the garage ramp about 75 feet (23.9m), where the van would be waiting. In the meantime, police were busy checking reporters' credentials. TV cameras were set up to

On November 24, 1963, with television cameras rolling, Jack "Ruby" Rubenstein (center) shot Lee Harvey Oswald. Here, Ruby holds a press conference at the start of his trial.

record the suspect's every move. The throng of people also included federal officials as well as locals friendly to law enforcement.

Tensions were high, despite the routine transfer. Then again, nothing was routine about Oswald. Finally, after 20 minutes, Oswald was taken downstairs in the elevator and led through the building. Fritz led the way, with detectives J.R. Leavelle and L.C. Graves on either side of him.

With cameras rolling and the world watching live on television, Oswald and his protectors appeared and started up the ramp to the van. Just then, a man jumped from the crowd of reporters, pressed a gun against Oswald's chest, and fired. Oswald grunted and fell to the ground. Police seized the assailant and hauled him into the building. The nation was stunned by what they had just witnessed and now craved the answer to a new question: Who shot the president's assassin?

In a matter of seconds, Dallas police knew the answer to that chilling question. Jack "Ruby" Rubenstein was well known to local law enforcement. As a Dallas nightclub owner, he was friendly to cops, often providing them with free drinks and entertainment on their nights off. During initial questioning Ruby claimed he shot Oswald because he felt pity for Kennedy's wife and children.

Meanwhile, Oswald was rushed to Parkland Hospital, where only two days before, Kennedy had expired and where Governor Connally was still recovering from his wounds. There, doctors discovered that Oswald had been shot just below the heart. The bullet damaged several vital arteries, and despite more than an hour of surgery Oswald died at 1:07 P.M.

Two Funerals

On the morning of Monday, November 25, Kennedy's flag-draped coffin was moved from the Capitol rotunda, where it had lain in state since Sunday. Over 300,000 Americans had filed past to pay their respects. Today, the leader of the free world would be carried to his final resting place.

The *Times* of London published a tribute by poet John Masefield:

> All generous hearts lament the leader killed,
> The young chief with the smile, the radiant face,
> The winning way that turned a wondrous race
> Into sublimer pathways, leading on. Grant to us
> life that though the man be gone. The promise of
> his spirit be fulfilled.[49]

At 10:41 A.M., the former First Lady, her face partially hidden by a black veil, and two of Kennedy's brothers, Robert and Edward, entered the rotunda and knelt before the president's coffin. After they said their final prayers, eight military pall bearers carried the casket outside and placed it on a caisson, a wagon used for formal occasions. Six matched gray horses then pulled it through the city toward the White House.

Three days before in Dallas, Texas, thousands had greeted their president with smiles and waves. For those lining the streets today, the greeting was a goodbye. Despite the bright and brisk November day, darkness had descended on the nation's capital. The events of the past days had confused and terrified many Americans; somehow it seemed that the United States itself was on the brink of disaster.

For many, it was television that connected them to one another, reflecting the sense of shared pity and terror that was gripping

After John F. Kennedy's funeral, Jacqueline Kennedy, six-year-old Caroline, and three-year-old John Jr. descended the cathedral steps. John-John saluted his father to the stirring sounds of "Hail to the Chief."

their lives. Millions watched as the funeral cortege reached 1600 Pennsylvania Avenue. Foreign dignitaries, including Charles de Gaulle of France, Prince Philip of Great Britain, and Haile Selassie of Ethiopia, passed the casket to pay their final respects. In all, 220 persons representing 92 nations attended the memorial.

Later, during the funeral mass at St. Matthew's Cathedral, Bishop Philip Hannan reached out to the mourners in attendance and to the nation at large. He used Kennedy's own words as tribute: "Ask not what your country can do for you—ask what you can do for your country."[50]

After the service was finished, Jacqueline Kennedy, six-year-old Caroline, and three-year-old John Jr. descended the cathedral steps. John-John, wearing a light blue coat, saluted his father to the stirring sounds of "Hail to the Chief."

The president's casket was once again placed on the caisson for its final journey. As described that day in the *New York Times,* "Behind it, Blackjack, the riderless gelding [horse] with the traditional reversed boots in stirrups, pranced and pawed nervously at the pavement."[51]

The gathered world leaders followed the sad train as it rode past the Lincoln Memorial, then onto the Memorial Bridge where it crossed the Potomac River into Arlington National Cemetery. The journey took more than an hour.

Once at the grave site, three cannons boomed 21 times in salute. The flag was removed from the coffin, folded, and handed to Mrs. Kennedy. Then she and Robert Kennedy lit the eternal flame that would forever mark the grave of President John F. Kennedy.

On the same day, to far less fanfare, Lee Harvey Oswald was buried at Rose Hill Memorial Burial Park in Fort Worth, Texas. In attendance were his wife, Marina; her young children, June and Rachel; Oswald's mother, Marguerite; and Oswald's brother, Robert, who paid for the burial and funeral. The inexpensive casket was paid for by the state.

The Oswald funeral was covered in all the newspapers as a sad contrast to that of the president's. But while Kennedy's burial was

"I'm just a patsy."

—Oswald implying that he did not kill the president, at least not by himself and without direction.

First Target?

In the months after Oswald's death, government agents and investigators found evidence that Kennedy's alleged assassin had attempted murder before. On the evening of April 10, 1963—only seven months before the president's assassination—General Edwin Walker was sitting in his study when a bullet shattered the window next to him. His arm was bleeding but he was otherwise uninjured.

Walker was just the kind of man Oswald hated—a staunch anti-Communist and an inveterate racist. It was discovered that not long before the assassination attempt on Walker, Oswald purchased a handgun and an Italian rifle through the mail. Oswald also began collecting information on the general, including photographs of his house and the intended hiding place for the rifle. A suspect in the attempt on Walker's life remained elusive until after Oswald's death, when an investigator questioned Marina Oswald and learned of her husband's detailed plans.

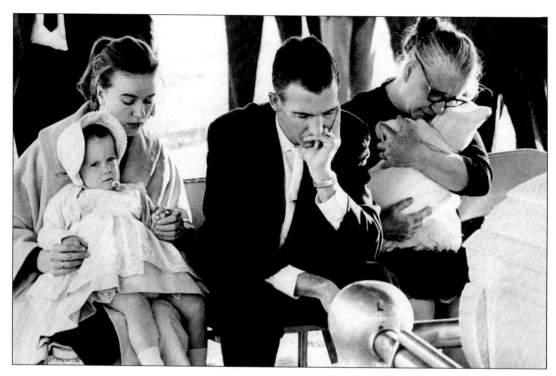

On the same day Kennedy was buried, Lee Harvey Oswald was buried at Rose Hill Memorial Burial Park in Fort Worth, Texas. In attendance were his wife, Marina; their young children, June and Rachel; Oswald's mother, Marguerite; and Oswald's brother, Robert, who paid for the burial and funeral.

a personal *and* a national tragedy with a tremendous outpouring of grief, the Oswald family had to bear their pain in silence.

Now, with the funerals at an end, the nation began to try to heal. But despite the evidence of Oswald's guilt, most Americans believed that Oswald did not act alone. The wound inflicted on November 22, 1963, would remain open. In truth, questions about Lee Harvey Oswald's motive and ability to carry out such a crime were only just beginning.

CHAPTER 3

Tangled Web: Calls of Conspiracy

If the past is any prologue, a suspicion of conspiracy was certainly warranted in 1963. The assassination of Abraham Lincoln in 1865 had been the work of many people. The original idea was to kidnap Lincoln and send him south into the Confederacy. But after that plan fell apart, assassin John Wilkes Booth stumbled into a bit of homicidal luck.

Lincoln would be attending a performance of the play *Our American Cousin* on April 14, Good Friday, at Ford's Theatre. The famous actor turned infamous assassin leaped at his chance. Later that night Booth crept into the president's unguarded box, put his .41-caliber Derringer to the back of the president's head, and pulled the trigger.

Then, with a large hunting knife in his other hand, Booth

slashed his way to the edge of the balcony and jumped to the stage. But his foot snagged on the American flag decorating the presidential box and he landed awkwardly, breaking his left leg.

The audience did not know what to make of the hubbub. Was this part of the play? Raising the knife above his head, Booth looked into the crowd, shouted "Sic semper tyrannus!" (Latin for "Thus always to tyrants!"), and limped from the stage and out the back door to his waiting horse.

But Booth had not acted alone. He had at least 10 helpers, one of whom, Lewis Paine, almost succeeded in killing Secretary of State William Seward in his bed. For 12 days, Booth's small network of Southern sympathizers aided him in escaping south. The proud assassin made it to Virginia, but he was killed by authorities in a barn, defiant to the last.

Ninety-eight years later, President Lyndon Johnson wanted to believe that Lee Harvey Oswald acted alone. He also feared the worst. "When something terrible happens in the life of a nation, there has to be a reason for it," says historian Evan Thomas, imagining Johnson's thinking. "It's not good enough to say some nut with a rifle killed JFK. It's such a monstrous thing that there must be a monster plot.[52]

In an effort to stem the tide of suspicion both within the government and in the public at large, Johnson ordered a thorough investigation. According to his aide Jack Valenti, the president "wanted a report that hopefully would allay the fears, the anxieties, and some of the conspiratorial darkness that was populating too many people's minds."[53]

Such an exhaustive investigation could mean the difference between war and peace. In the 1950s and 1960s, tensions were high between the United States and the Soviet Union. A cold war was

The CIA's mission statement says that "We accomplish what others cannot accomplish and go where others cannot go."

being fought in which each country stockpiled nuclear weapons in an attempt to frighten the other and consolidate power.

In 1962 President Kennedy and Soviet premier Nikita Khrushchev had narrowly avoided launching an all-out nuclear war over the perceived presence of Soviet missiles in Cuba. Now, millions of lives were potentially at stake again. Johnson sincerely hoped that the Soviets would not be implicated in Kennedy's death. If they were, it could be the start of World War III.

The Warren Commission

The report Johnson commissioned under Supreme Court chief justice Earl Warren had two goals. The first was to "settle the mood in the United States," according to historian Robert Goldberg. The second was to "dispel any rumors of foreign intrigue,"[54] particularly Soviet involvement.

Such thoughts were naturally on the minds of many Americans, especially after word of Oswald's 1959 defection to the Soviet Union came to light. In fact, much of Oswald's life was a mystery at the time, leaving open a variety of possible connections to secret organizations or rogue nations.

Over the course of 10 grueling months, the Warren Commission (pictured) probed the Kennedy killing, interviewing 25,000 people, including Oswald's wife, mother, and brother, and carefully reviewing 3,000 pieces of evidence.

Over the course of 10 grueling months, the 7-member Warren Commission probed the Kennedy killing, interviewing 25,000 people, including Oswald's wife, mother, and brother, and carefully reviewing 3,000 pieces of evidence. According to the 888-page final document, published in September 1964, the bullets that killed the president came from Oswald's rifle; the palm print on the rifle stock belonged to him; and fingerprints on the boxes surrounding the sniper's perch were his too.

The commission determined that three shots were fired. One missed its target altogether, but two shots hit the president. One was the fatal shot to the brain; the other, a single bullet—shot from behind—passed through the rear of Kennedy's throat or upper back, then struck Connally and lodged in his thigh. The final determination of the commission was that Lee Harvey Oswald acted alone and was neither aided nor funded by others.

The Warren Commission's findings became—and are today—the U.S. government's final word on the subject of the assassination. But a majority of Americans were not buying the commission's explanations. Instead, inconsistencies and omissions in the report are often pointed to as sure signs that the complete story of November 22, 1963, has never been told.

Magic Bullet I

A major criticism of the Warren Commission's work revolves around the number of bullets fired in Dealey Plaza. The commission determined that there were three: The first missed; the second struck Kennedy in the lower throat area and passed into Connally's body; and the third and fatal shot shattered the back of the president's skull. Most conspiracy theorists dispute this chain of events.

Commission Exhibit (or CE) 399 is a touchstone for the

"It's not good enough to say that some nut with a rifle killed JFK."

—Historian Evan Thomas commenting on those crying conspiracy.

conspiracy-minded. This "magic bullet," as it has been called, is credited with injuring two men. But based on its disputed point of entry, was that possible? Investigator and author Henry Hurt says the very idea defies logic: "One must accept that in wounding President Kennedy and Governor Connally, this remarkable bullet traversed seven layers of skin, pierced through muscle tissue, and smashed bones. The bullet then emerged practically unscathed."[55]

Furthermore, he argues that there is "no proof of how many shots were fired."[56] He chides the Warren Commission on this point, suggesting that the evidence of three shots is based only on the three spent cartridges found in the Texas School Book Depository.

Hurt and other skeptics have also doubted Oswald's ability to fire three shots in only 8.3 seconds (or much less) with, what author Kurtz describes as an "ancient, bolt-action rifle."[57] This assertion has given rise to the idea that Oswald was not the only shooter that day.

Also controversial is the conflicting information on where the magic bullet entered Kennedy's body. While the Warren Commission report states that "a bullet had entered the base of the back of his neck slightly to the right of the spine,"[58] bullet holes in the president's shirt strongly suggest the bullet entered about six inches lower, in his back.

In 1997 former president Gerald Ford, a member of the Warren Commission in 1964, admitted to changing the commission report to focus on the neck area. Conspiracy enthusiasts wonder if Ford's revision was written to protect the magic bullet hypothesis and thus the findings of the Warren Commission. Ford claimed that his change was only made in an effort to be more precise.

Pictured is
the grassy
knoll and
Elm Street
in Dealey
Plaza. Some
believe that
there was
a second
shooter posi-
tioned on
the grassy
knoll.

Autopsy

Many have also faulted the Warren Commission for not fully investigating reports of at least one other possible shooter. Suspicion
derives from the autopsy done on Kennedy at Parkland Hospital.

According to conspiracy supporters, including Kurtz, at least
seven medical specialists—nurses, doctors, and technicians—
stated that Kennedy's fatal head wound was the result of a shot
made from the front, not the back. If proven, this would potentially undermine the Warren Commission's conclusion that Oswald shot the president from the sixth floor of the book depository, behind Kennedy.

Kurtz also reports that nonmedical observers—Secret Service
agents Roy Kellerman, William Greer, and Clint Hill—also saw
an entry rather than an exit wound in the president's throat. The

mystery deepens, says Kurtz, who has pored over thousands of documents in 40 years of research, in that "the autopsy photographs depict no such hole."[59]

The difference between what witnesses saw that day and the photographic evidence available remains unexplained. But David Mantik, a physician who spent hours studying the autopsy pictures in 1963, has no doubts. "The photographic collection has been deliberately manipulated to mislead,"[60] he says. Mantik bases his theory on precise measurements he took of the wounds in the available photographs. These measurements, says Mantik, coupled with "the insertion of a metallic fragment in the back of the skull to make it appear that a shot struck Kennedy from behind,"[61] only raise more perplexing questions. Also, statements made by the physicians attending to the president placed the location of the fatal head wound very low in the back of the head. But official photographs put the wound four inches higher, near the top of the head.

Unfortunately, many autopsy photographs were confiscated by government agents on the day of the assassination. The Kennedy family received the photographs soon after and in 1966 gave them to the National Archives with the understanding that their use would be restricted. To this day, while a handful of Kennedy autopsy photographs are readily available, others are said to be closely guarded and rarely seen.

The Grassy Knoll

If, indeed, Kennedy was shot at least once from the front, then the shots must have been fired from the grassy knoll, that patch of land between the railroad tower and the book depository. Julia Ann Mercer waited in a traffic jam on the day of the assassination.

"The photographic collection has been deliberately manipulated to mislead."

— Dr. David Mantik on his doubts about the autopsy photos.

Afterward, she said she had seen two men in a green pickup truck. One removed a gun case from the rear and headed off to the grassy knoll. Later, she identified one man as Jack Ruby and the other as Lee Oswald. Her testimony was quickly dismissed by Warren Commission investigators as being too outlandish.

But other reports of suspicious behavior on the grassy knoll are not as easily disproved. Immediately after the assassination, police officer Joe Marshall Smith was approached by a screaming woman who told him, "They're shooting the president from the bushes."[62] Smith checked the bushes and then bumped into a man at a fence that separated the grassy knoll from a parking lot. On seeing a policeman with his pistol drawn, the stranger produced a secret service badge. Smith let the stranger go on his way.

At the time of the assassination, college student Cheryl McKinnon was standing on the grassy knoll when she heard three shots come from behind her. "Puffs of white smoke still hung in the air in small patches," McKinnon says, "but no one was visible."[63]

CIA Connection

Just who was that Secret Service agent who flashed his badge to Smith? He has never been identified. But if the man was a government agent—which is open to debate—what was he doing near the grassy knoll? Was he to blame for the puffs of white smoke—presumably from a gun—that McKinnon spoke of? Most important, was this man acting as protection against a would-be attack on the president, or was he somehow involved in the attack?

Speculation into government involvement in the Kennedy assassination is widespread. Most of it still centers around Oswald, but in this version of events Oswald was either only one of multiple shooters connected to the CIA (Central Intelligence Agency) or a patsy, as Oswald himself claimed, meaning he was not directly involved in the shooting. He was set up to look like the murderer, this theory claims, but others did the actual shooting.

John Newman, author of *Oswald and the CIA*, is certain of one thing: The CIA had a great interest in Oswald "from the day he defected to the Soviet Union until the day he was murdered in the basement of the Dallas City jail."[64] Newman documents the secret files he claims the CIA had on Oswald. And while he will not go so far as to suggest that Oswald was an agent for the CIA, Newman does not rule it out.

In 1964, in front of the Warren Commission, CIA director John A. McCone denied any relationship with Oswald. He "was never associated or connected directly or indirectly in any way whatso-ever with the Agency."[65]

In 1978, when the investigation was reopened by the House Select Committee on Assassination (HSCA), the CIA's opinion on the matter had shifted slightly. The agency admitted that although "there was no indication"[66] of an Oswald/CIA relationship, the agency's use of deep cover—top secret and complex techniques— might make an existing relationship unknowable.

Is such testimony the sure sign of a cover-up? It is impossible to know, but possible to believe. The CIA is responsible for all overseas intelligence gathering, meaning their job is to spy on suspected terrorists or dangerous governments. Much of their work, by its very nature, is secretive and rarely spoken of in pub-lic. Agents must often work with mysterious, even underhanded people—people like Oswald.

What is clear is that in late September and early October 1963, Oswald traveled to Mexico City, Mexico. What he did there or with whom is unknown. The Warren Commission did little in-

"[He] was never associated . . . with the Agency."

— CIA director John A. McCone, denying any relationship with Oswald.

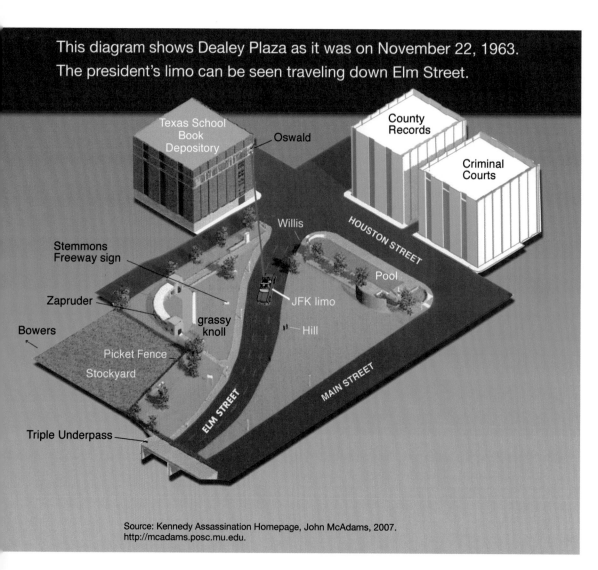

This diagram shows Dealey Plaza as it was on November 22, 1963. The president's limo can be seen traveling down Elm Street.

Texas School Book Depository

Oswald

County Records

Criminal Courts

Willis

HOUSTON STREET

Stemmons Freeway sign

Pool

Zapruder

JFK limo

grassy knoll

Bowers

Hill

Picket Fence

Stockyard

ELM STREET

MAIN STREET

Triple Underpass

Source: Kennedy Assassination Homepage, John McAdams, 2007.
http://mcadams.posc.mu.edu.

vestigation into this hole in Oswald's profile. But critics of the official report point to the trip, and another longer one that Oswald made to his hometown of New Orleans, as evidence that he may have been meeting with secret agents or government operatives.

In 1959 the Cuban government of President Fulgencio Batista was overthrown by Communist revolutionaries led by Fidel Castro (pictured). While Batista's government was friendly to the United States, Castro's was not. The idea of overthrowing Castro and installing a government more in tune with the interests of the United States became appealing to Kennedy, making some believe that Castro may have been involved in Kennedy's assassination.

One government report titled "Lee Harvey Oswald, the CIA, and Mexico City" tells of an Oswald impersonator—a fake—appearing south of the border. Oswald or someone claiming to be him appeared at both the Cuban and Soviet embassies. Apparently, the man wanted a travel visa to Havana, Cuba, after which he would fly to Moscow. Embassy employees had different recollections of the man they met, with some identifying Oswald and others describing a different man.

After his trial Jack
Ruby hinted at his
hand in a larger
conspiracy, suggesting
that all of the details
of the Kennedy
assassination and
subsequent events
might never be
known.

Entry or Exit?

Perhaps the most hotly contested aspect of the assassination—apart from the "magic bullet"—is Kennedy's front neck wound. Initial examiners Drs. Malcolm Perry, Kemp Clark, Charles Crenshaw, and James Carrico described seeing a small, round entry wound in the president's throat during their initial exam. If the hole was indeed one of entry, then Oswald—shooting from behind Kennedy—could not have acted alone. Evidence does support the notion that President Johnson wanted to find

On October 10, 1963, according to Kurtz, the CIA relayed an unusual message to the FBI (Federal Bureau of Investigation), the State Department, and the navy. It described a man quite unlike Lee Harvey Oswald appearing at the foreign embassies: "The American was described as approximately 35 years old, with an athletic build, about six feet tall with a receding hairline."[67] Oswald was 24, skinny, and only 5'4" (1.6m) in height. Kurtz also claims that the CIA made "efforts to steer the Warren Commission away from any path that would a single assassin. What is less clear is to what lengths, if any, Secret Service agents went in convincing the autopsy doctors to change their original story.

Author Michael L. Kurtz reveals that before the doctors testified before the Warren Commission, a government agent paid them visits and eventually cajoled them into believing that the wound was one of entry not exit. Other medical staff at Parkland Hospital apparently disagreed, still certain that it was an entry wound. Complicating matters was the tracheotomy performed by Perry to try and revive the dying Kennedy. The procedure involved making the controversial bullet hole larger, thus destroying any possibility of a definitive answer.

link Oswald to the intelligence agency."[68]

Between 1993 and 1995, 2 million pages of CIA and FBI documents related to the Kennedy assassination were released. "These files clearly show that there's hardly an intelligence agency that did not have an interest in Lee Harvey Oswald," says investigator W. Scott Malone. "The FBI was concerned that an impostor might be using his papers to sneak into the United States. And the CIA had both a positive and a counterintelligence interest."[69]

Castro, Cuba, and the Soviets

If the critics of the Warren Report are right, the question still remains: Why would Oswald have been hired by or involved with the CIA? And what interest would American agents have in the death of a president? Speculation typically centers on a covert CIA operation in Cuba called the Bay of Pigs invasion.

In 1959 the Cuban government of President Fulgencio Batista was overthrown by Communist revolutionaries led by Fidel Castro. While Batista's government was friendly to the United States, Castro's was not. Over the course of two years, a war of words flew between the Kennedy administration and the now Communist nation. The idea of overthrowing Castro and installing a government more in tune with the interests of the United States became appealing to Kennedy.

On March 10, 1961, American military advisers briefed defense secretary Robert McNamara and told him that a small invasion force of 1,200–1,500 men was prepared to slip onto the island. The force would be made up primarily of men who had been forced to flee Cuba when Castro came to power. These exiles would be assisted by the CIA. Kennedy agreed to the secret plan, but he insisted that "U.S. assistance would be less obvious."[70]

The Cuban exiles were anxious for a chance to bring Castro down; Kennedy wanted to support them but also feared what failure could bring. If the Soviets, archenemy of the United States, found out about the plan, they might try to protect Castro and threaten the United States. If Kennedy decided to scrap the plan, the exiles might accuse him of being too soft on Castro.

The president went back and forth with his decision. New plans were drawn up, but still Kennedy hesitated. He "reserved the right to call off the plan even up to 24 hours prior"[71] to the invasion.

When asked at a news conference whether an invasion of Cuba by U.S. forces was imminent, Kennedy said, "There will not be, under any conditions, an intervention in Cuba by the United States Armed Forces."[72]

Two days after unsuccessful bombings on three Cuban airfields, a small force landed at the Bay of Pigs, an inlet in the Zapata region of Cuba. The April 17 invasion quickly became a disaster, as the exiles were greeted by Castro's Soviet tanks and 20,000 of his soldiers. According to historian Robert Dallek, "The outgunned and outmanned invaders faced dying on the beaches in a hopeless fight or surrender."[73] Most of the 1,400 invaders chose to surrender.

Soon after the Kennedy assassination, skeptics put forth three theories related to the Bay of Pigs fiasco. One focuses on the Cuban exiles who felt abandoned and undersupported by the United States. In this version of events, the exiles wreaked revenge on Kennedy—through Oswald—for the Bay of Pigs disaster by having him killed.

The second theory suggests that members of the CIA, FBI, and the military wanted Kennedy dead because of his weakness and indecision in relation to the Soviet Union. Another tantalizing possibility is that Castro himself, furious at the attempt to destroy him, enlisted secret agents of his own and had the president killed.

Johnson was certain this was the case. "Kennedy tried to get Castro, and Castro got Kennedy first," says former Johnson aide Joseph A. Califano Jr. "President Johnson went to his grave believing that Castro was behind Lee Harvey Oswald's assassination of John Kennedy."[74]

In 1978 an American delegation investigating Kennedy's murder went to Cuba and asked Castro directly whether he killed Kennedy. Castro denied it, saying how foolish it would have been. "That would have been the perfect pretext for the United States to invade our country," said Castro, "which is what I have tried to prevent for all these years."[75] While the Cuban leader may have been lying, no evidence has yet tied him to any plot.

As for the Russians and Oswald's three-year sojourn in the Soviet Union, former KGB (Soviet secret police) agent Yuri Nosenko also denies a connection. In Nosenko's opinion, Oswald's shaky personality made a deal with the Soviets impossible. "He was a nobody," says Nosenko. "He was a tumbleweed."[76]

Another agent, Vacheslav Nikonow, remembers that Oswald "was not interested in Marxism. He didn't attend any Marxist classes. He didn't read any Marxist literature and he didn't attend even the labor union meetings. So the question was, what was he doing there?"[77]

Kennedy, Oswald, and the Mob

Jack Ruby, the nightclub owner who shot and killed Oswald on national TV, claimed he shot Oswald because he pitied Kennedy's children and wife. "I did it for the people of America,"[78] said Ruby. Yet, despite his affection for Kennedy and his family, there is no evidence that Ruby watched his beloved president's motorcade pass by. Then again, Ruby, known to police and mobsters alike, was a hard man to pin down.

Since 1963 rumors have tied Ruby to the Mafia. Could Ruby have killed Oswald to keep him from squealing to the police about the mob's involvement in Kennedy's murder? If so, what did the mob have against the president of the United States?

After 1961, attorney general Robert "Bobby" Kennedy cut what legal corners he could in bringing mobsters to justice. One of Kennedy's first targets was New Orleans crime boss Carlos Marcello. In April of that year, the attorney general ordered agents to arrest Marcello and deport him to Guatemala. There, Marcello was dropped in a remote jungle.

When a furious Marcello returned to the United States, he made his hatred of John and Bobby Kennedy clear to all who would listen. But Marcello was only one of many mobsters who were incensed by the government crackdown on the family business. In other words, few Mafia families would have shed tears over the death of the president or his brother.

But did one of them actually pay to have a hit put on the highest elected official in the land, and then also put a hit on his assassin? There is little hard evidence, only conjecture. Ruby's rabbi Hillel Silverman takes Ruby at his word. "He denied it vehemently again and again and again," says Silverman. He goes on to quote Ruby himself: "'I'll swear on this bible. I had nothing to do with anybody else.'"[79] Even if Ruby did know something, Dallas reporter Hugh Aynesworth says, "This is a man, if he knew anything, he'd tell somebody within one block. He wanted to be important."[80]

The true story may never be told. Ruby died in jail after being convicted of Oswald's murder, and few of those connected with the mob in those days are still alive. And those who are, are not talking.

G. Robert Blakey, chief counsel to the House Select Committee on Assassination, said this about the fiery nightclub owner: "The murder of Oswald by Jack Ruby had all the earmarks of an organized-crime hit, an action to silence the assassin, so he could not reveal the conspiracy."[81]

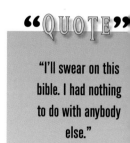

"QUOTE"

"I'll swear on this bible. I had nothing to do with anybody else."

—Jack Ruby confessing to Rabbi Hillel Silverman.

CHAPTER 4

Science and Suspicion

In the 45 years since the Kennedy assassination, scientific methods have greatly improved. Twenty-first-century technology can now be used to investigate a twentieth-century crime. Such advances provide investigators with renewed hope that the world's most infamous murder case can finally be put to rest.

While the major pieces of the puzzle remain the same, computer-enhanced imagery, more sophisticated ballistics tests, and sound amplification offer new ways of looking at the pieces. How people fit them together, though, has not changed much. For lone-gunman supporters these methods mostly reinforce what they already believe: Oswald acted alone. For the conspiracy-minded, the results offer proof of a massive cover-up.

Two Men Up There

Immediately after the Kennedy shooting, some witnesses claimed they saw two men on the sixth floor of the book depository. Such a finding would be clear proof of a conspiracy. At 12:23 P.M., moments before the assassination, amateur filmmaker Charles Bronson stood across the street from the depository. While waiting for the president's motorcade he panned the building with his camera.

Thirty years later, image-processing analyst Robert Gonsalves enhanced Bronson's film and took a closer look. What he found was initially startling. "The left window, when you look at a single frame, appears to have a person standing there. But when we processed the image to reduce the grain noise, we found that all of the images throughout the frame look approximately the same." Grain noise is the random pieces of color and unwanted flecks of texture that can distort the photographed image. In the end, Gonsalves's final determination was, "That is not anybody walking around. That's grain noise walking around."[82]

Another amateur film, this one by bystander Robert Hughes, moves right as the president's limousine passes before the book depository. The sixth-floor window, right next to the shooter's, appears to have a human form in it. "When we ran the enhanced film in motion, that human form disappears and we conclude there is no human form in that window," says image analyst Francis Corbett. "We do also conclude that there is movement in the sixth floor corner window, indicating the presence of a person."[83]

Further study of Hughes's film indicates that only seven seconds before the first shot, something or someone moves in the corner window. Harold Norman, hanging out of a fifth-floor window and waving to the passing president heard the gunfire. "We

Did You Know?

At the Texas School Book Depository, Oswald earned $1.25 per hour. While the pay was poor, he said he enjoyed working with books.

was sitting on the fifth floor, directly under the sixth floor windows," he said. "The shots came from above and there was a gun and the shots were sounding, 'Boom! Click, click. Boom! Click, click. Boom! Click, click.' So there was three shots fired right up over us when we were sitting on the fifth floor."[84]

Combining technology and eyewitness accounts, experts agree that Oswald was the only one on the sixth floor at the time of the shooting. But whether those shots came from his rifle or even from the depository is another matter entirely.

Magic Bullet II

ABC News consultant Dale Myers spent 25 years studying the Kennedy assassination and finds a disparity. "90% of what is out there is conspiracy-oriented," says Myers. You can talk about all the theories you want. This thing happened only one way."[85] Myers, a computer animator, devised a simulation of the assassination reconstructed from and superimposed over the Zapruder film.

First, Myers created a scale model of Dealey Plaza exactly as it was on November 22, 1963. With a click of the mouse, a viewer can watch the assassination unfold from any angle. Then, Myers placed computer-generated figures in the limousine to represent Kennedy and Connally. The next step was to painstakingly identify the movements of both men and synchronize them with Zapruder's footage. In other words, the computer version had to exactly match the only known film of the assassination.

In the film, frame 133 is the first in which Kennedy is visible. According to Myers, close study reveals that it is at frame 160 where the first shot takes place. While the conspiracy-minded might quibble with this conclusion, it is at this moment that Connally's head swivels from his left to his right side. The governor is trying to see where the sound—the shot—has come from.

At this point the limousine passed behind a freeway sign; the president and governor are hidden momentarily. As the car becomes visible again something has changed. "Both men are reacting simultaneously,"[86] says Myers. The president reaches for his lower throat and Connally reacts. This occurs between frames 223 and 224 of Zapruder's film. The precise moment of Kennedy's throat-reach is impossible to ascertain, but Myers thinks he is pretty close.

In his computer rendering Myers also pinpoints the exact location of the men's bodies at the time of the second shot. From this he concludes that one bullet—the second—did pass through and injure both men. Their positions at the moment of impact—Kennedy directly behind and higher, Connally turned sharply to his right—make it very possible for the so-called magic bullet to do extraordinary damage. "It's not a magic bullet at all," Myers concludes. "It's not even a single-bullet theory. It's a single-bullet fact."[87]

Posner agrees with Myers's basic conclusion. "Four government commissions all concluded it was a straight line right through the two men," he says. "There's no question that a single bullet could inflict all . . . wounds on both the President and the Governor and emerge in very good condition."[88]

Finally, Myers projects a line backward from the Connally wound, through the Kennedy wound, to where he is certain the shot came from: the Texas School Book Depository. Posner agrees with Myers's final analysis:

> There were only two shots that struck President Kennedy. Both came from the rear. Four government investigations all came to the same conclusion—the Warren Commission

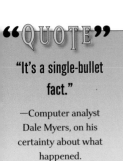

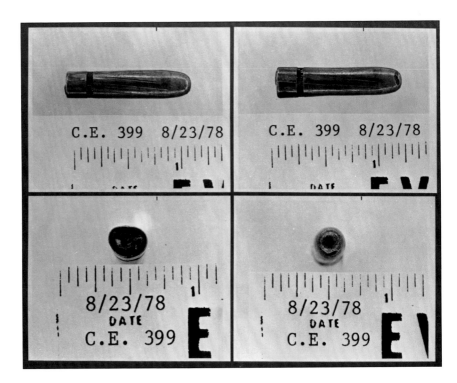

(Top row) This is the bullet that was found at Parkland Hospital. Tests confirmed it came from Oswald's rifle, but no one is sure whether it came from Connally's or Kennedy's stretcher. (Bottom row) Seen here is the "magic bullet."

in the '60s, in 1968 the Clark panel set by Attorney General Ramsey Clark, in the '70s the Rockefeller Commission and finally, in the late '70s, the House Select Committee, with the largest forensics panel reexamining the evidence.[89]

Dr. Robert Shaw of Parkland Hospital, though, stated that Kennedy's entrance wound was 1.5 centimeters, not the 3.0 centimeters Oswald's rifle would have inflicted. Shaw also said the bullet's angle through the men's bodies was too circuitous or roundabout. If both men sat upright, Shaw suggested, the bullet could not have traveled through both of them. The debate in this critical matter will rage on.

Ballistics

Much controversy also surrounds the condition of the bullets, especially the one that struck both men. Later known as the "magic bullet," it was found on a stretcher in Parkland Hospital in the aftermath of Kennedy's death. No one seems to know how it got there. Did it fall out of Connally's thigh as he was wheeled into the emergency room? Was it removed by a surgeon and dropped in transit to the lab? Or, as the suspicious suggest, did Jack Ruby plant it there as a way of framing the man he would kill two days later?

Henry Hurt in his 1985 book *Reasonable Doubt* called into question the Warren Commission's ballistics tests on the found bullet. How could a bullet, he asked, that passes through two men, striking ribs and flesh, remain so intact? "The only damage to the bullet's nose is the small sliver removed by the FBI for testing."[90] During the Warren Commission investigation, three tests were done using the caliber of bullet found in Connally's thigh. The first used cotton, the second used a goat carcass, and the third used a human cadaver. In each case the bullets were far more damaged than the bullet that passed through Kennedy's and Connally's bodies. Hurt's research lends at least a sliver of support to the idea that Ruby (or someone else) dropped the bullet on the stretcher.

But at least one man takes issue with Hurt's basic conclusion. "The problem was that people were denying that there was any damage," says Dr. John Lattimer, who also studied the evidence closely. "They were calling it pristine. And it's absolutely, positively not pristine. It's flat."[91] In other words, Lattimer reports that the bullet's nose shows clear signs of damage. The question remains: Is this the bullet that passed through two bodies, striking bone and ending in Connally's leg? Depending on whom you ask, the answer is bound to be different.

Regardless of Lattimer's rebuttal, Hurt remains unconvinced about the bullet itself. "There is not a shred of solid, undisputed evidence," he wrote, "to show that the bullet [fired from Oswald's rifle] had anything at all to do with the shooting of President Kennedy."[92] House Select Committee ballistics expert Larry Sturdivan disagrees. In a 2003 interview, Sturdivan said that the tiny scratches "made as this bullet spun down the rifle barrel exactly matched"[93] the bullet fired from Oswald's rifle.

In the spring of 2007 a team of scientists took another look. They, like Hurt, challenged the bullet analysis used by government investigators to conclude that Oswald alone fired the two bullets that killed the president.

The scientists' article, written for the *Annals of Applied Statistics*, said, "the evidence used to rule out a second assassin is fundamentally flawed."[94] The study itself was commissioned by Texas A&M University, where a team of scientists used techniques unavailable 40 years ago. After much study and analysis, they concluded that the bullet fragments involved in the assassination were not as rare as once thought. Therefore, say these experts, the bullets that struck the president may have come from a gun other than Oswald's.

Although the study is not conclusive, leading forensic expert

"With a probability of 95% there was indeed a shot fired from the grassy knoll."

—Forensic scientists, dropping a bombshell in 1978.

Back and to the Left

Much has been made of the movement of President Kennedy's head upon receiving the fatal shot. The Zapruder film clearly shows a lurch backward and to the left. What this motion says about where the bullet came from, though, is inconclusive. It seems to follow that a bullet-pierced body will continue traveling in the direction of the fired shot. If, then, Kennedy was shot from the front, his head would travel backward, as the film clearly shows. But other experts have concluded that it is impossible to predict a body's reaction at the moment of impact.

Cliff Spiegelman says that "by properly reanalyzing the bullet fragments, our nation has a chance to shatter a myth about the JFK assassination."[95] The myth to which Spiegelman is referring is that one man was responsible for Kennedy's murder.

Heard on the Radio

Scientific analysis was used again in 1976 when a House Select Committee was formed to revisit the Kennedy assassination and the Warren Commission's findings. The Bay of Pigs plot had become public knowledge the year before, and the nation still teemed with conspiracy-related theories. Many believed the Warren Commission itself had been part of a massive cover-up by a corrupt government. Headed by attorney G. Robert Blakey, the House Committee combed through the evidence again, called old and new witnesses to the stand, and sought to get to the bottom of the mystery once and for all. "We made it our central program," says Blakey, "to see what might have changed since 1963."[96] But after two exhaustive years, the conclusion was that the Warren Commission, despite numerous flaws in its final report, had come to the right conclusion. Not enough evidence existed to connect anyone but Oswald to the death of the thirty-fifth president.

But then, in the final week of the hearing a team of scientists dropped a bombshell: "With a probability of 95% or better," they said, "there was indeed a shot fired from the grassy knoll."[97] The evidence the team presented appeared not only sound but decisive.

The shooting of Kennedy had been inadvertently recorded, the scientists said, when a motorcycle policeman's radio was left on. If true, the fourth shot heard on the tape would prove a conspiracy existed, since Oswald—in little more than eight seconds or less—would not have had time to fire one more round.

This was it, the literal smoking gun. It proved what so many had believed for so long. Or did it? Officer H.B. McLain was in the motorcade that day. It was his radio that recorded the shots. But for the scientific team's theory to hold, McLain must have been at the corner of Houston and Elm Streets to pick up those crucial sounds. It was here that Kennedy's limousine turned and drove past the book depository.

McLain was interviewed by the House Select Committee. He clearly recalled his position at the time of the first shot, and he was certain he was not where the committee told him he had to be to make the theory work. The committee did not believe him. "They just assumed [the radio] was mine," says McLain. "I don't care what they say. It wasn't mine."[98]

Posner agrees. "The National Academy of Sciences reviewed their work and found a multitude of errors and omissions, the most serious of which was that the time that the Select Committee experts thought the shots were being fired was the wrong time. It was actually one minute after the assassination had taken place."[99]

Dr. Robert Shaw stated that Kennedy's entrance wound was 1.5 centimeters, not the 3.0 centimeters Oswald's rifle would have inflicted. Pictured is Oswald's rifle shortly after it was discovered by investigators.

Zapruder Fake

Another key piece of data has also gotten a closer look in recent years. The film made by Abraham Zapruder was for many years considered beyond reproach. After all, the Warren Commission based its primary conclusions on this vital footage. Then, in 2003 James H. Fetzer, Distinguished McKnight University Professor at the University of Minnesota, published *The Great Zapruder Film Hoax*. His book contains essays by a variety of scholars on the possibility that the film was tampered with.

Mostly at issue for these investigators is the belief that the Kennedy limousine and the spectators standing near the car do not

match. In other words, say the skeptics, the whole film was manufactured. On his Web site, Fetzer claims that whoever forged the film simply cut-and-pasted the background onto the footage showing the president's car. Related to this is the film's speed, which Fetzer says varies from person to person. "Jackie Kennedy seems to move quite normally," [100] he writes. But in his estimation, the same cannot be said for onlookers, some of whom appear to be looking behind the president rather than directly at him.

The forgers, according to Fetzer, used three techniques to cover up their mistakes: First, they made it appear that Zapruder jiggled his camera so details are hard to follow. Next, they kept the film from public view for 12 years, hoping to bury any inconsistencies, at least for a while. (Although the Warren Commission viewed the Zapruder film, it was not shown on TV.) Finally, they published the still photographs from the film in poor-quality black and white.

Also at issue is the moment of impact. As the fatal shot strikes Kennedy his head moves back and to the left. Does that not mean the assassin shot the president from the front? While the Zapruder film provides no definitive evidence in this regard, Fetzer also references assassination writer David Lifton, who is certain that the head wound shown in the Zapruder film and the wound seen during the autopsy do not match.

Beyond the famous film, Fetzer has spent the last 30 years pursuing the truth, and he strongly questions much of the lone-gunman evidence. Especially unlikely, he says, are Posner's conclusions and his scientific methods. He criticizes Posner's "penchant for selective use of evidence."[101] He is particularly skeptical about Posner's investigation of the bullet holes in Kennedy's shirt.

What Posner forgets, says Fetzer, is the quality of the clothes

Kennedy wore. The difference in opinion stems from the location of the back hole—was it higher, near the neck, or 5.5 inches (14cm) lower? Posner suggests the hole was high up, but that Kennedy's clothes bunched; therefore, the lower hole was created.

Fetzer decries this theory by making the point that Kennedy's clothes were finely tailored and unlikely to bunch. Also suspect to Fetzer was the autopsy itself, which was performed by two doctors who had never performed one on a gunshot victim.

The overall conclusion Fetzer draws, based on his own scientific investigation, is a shocking one: "JFK was hit at least four times; once in the throat from the front; once in the back from behind; and twice in the head, once from the back and once from the front."[102] When Fetzer adds in the separate shots that struck Connally, he concludes that 8, 9, or 10 shots were fired from 6 different locations.

Straight from the Hart

Paul J. Hart, like Fetzer, considers himself a serious skeptic on the official version of events. But Hart keeps most of his opinions on the Kennedy assassination to himself these days. He has no Web site, he has written no books on the subject, and, as he will quickly tell you, "I've never made a dime on this."[103] Instead, Hart is one of thousands of amateur sleuths who have studied the assassination over many years, collecting artifacts and information that he believes prove his point.

Hart's interest in the subject began—like so many—on that sunny day in November. At the time, he was a 15-year-old high school student and a dedicated Kennedy fan. "He [Kennedy] was so young, like Diana [the Princess of Wales, killed in 1997]. We never thought he was going to die."[104]

More than a decade after the assassination, Hart and a friend made a trip to the National Archives in Washington, D.C. On a lark the young men asked the curator if they could see Oswald's rifle and the magic bullet. To their surprise, they were told to return at 4:30.

Later that day Hart and his friend were led into the archives' basement, where the curator held the infamous rifle in his hands and they got to look through the sight. Afterward, the two closely scrutinized the "magic bullet." When Hart speaks of that special day, there is still a twinkle in his eye. In the years to come, that once-in-a-lifetime moment would play at least some role in Hart's chosen profession: American history teacher. He has taught the subject to high school students now for 33 years, inspiring many of them to become history teachers.

"I've never been someone who wanted to exonerate Oswald," he says. But based on his close study, "There's a good chance he didn't fire one shot."[105] Hart's primary evidence is what he believes to be definitive proof that more than 3 bullets were fired at Kennedy's motorcade. He is especially intrigued by a man named James Tague, who stood 520 feet (158.5m) from the Texas School Book Depository. Tague had parked his car and stood under the southern end of the triple underpass—in front and to the left of Kennedy's car. One of the shots—which one is unclear—struck the curb nearby and sent fragments of cement into Tague's face.

When questioned afterward by the Dallas police, Tague said he did not know which shot hit the curb. Such uncertainty has led some conspiracy-hunters to believe that Tague's experience proves that the Warren Commission Report was again wrong. There had to be more than three shots, proving that a conspiracy took place.

The Warren Commission barely investigated Tague's story until July 1964. They concluded that the bullet "cannot be identified conclusively with any of the three shots fired."[106] Since that time, lone-gunman supporters have put forward that Tague's minor injuries were the result of the first missed shot. Hart does not buy it.

According to his calculations, five shots were fired that day: The first caused JFK's back wound, which was in the Warren Commission Report but is omitted from the drawings. This was followed by the shot from the front, which caused the controversial but unproven throat wound. Connally sustained five bullet wounds. Hart, like many others, is convinced that the bullets that struck Kennedy could not also have hit Connally. The fourth bullet, says Hart, missed the president's limousine and is probably the one that caused the injury to James Tague. The fifth and final shot hit Kennedy in the head.

Though convinced of a conspiracy, Hart is willing to listen to any new or more accurate evidence. Still, he has particular scorn for the Warren Commission. "They knew what they were doing. They reduced the number of shots."[107] They had a preordained theory, he says. The goal was to pin the crime solely on Oswald because otherwise the nation might be on the brink of war.

There is a large audience out there that craves such maverick material. What drives contemporary detectives like Hart and Fetzer is an incessant desire to get to the bottom of things. Hart, though, freely admits the bottom may forever remain undiscovered. "It's the one thing," he says, "that the more I learn the less I seem to know."[108]

CHAPTER 5

Case Closed . . . or Is It?

As recently as the summer of 2001, a poll revealed that 68 percent of Americans still believe that John F. Kennedy's death was the result of a conspiracy. For them, the Warren Commission report remains a fatally flawed document. "Serious researchers easily exposed many of the commission's shortcomings," writes Kurtz, "and provided their readers and audiences with ample evidence of an assassination conspiracy." [109] This skepticism has value, as new investigations occasionally reveal fresh angles that might bring a definitive conclusion closer.

On the other hand, the mystery surrounding the most famous murder in American history is self-perpetuating; it feeds on itself and is unlikely to fade anytime soon. For those who hunger for stories of secret agents, corrupt government officials, and international intrigue, the Kennedy assassination encourages plenty of debate and various ways of attacking the evidence.

JFK Goes Hollywood

Controversy over the assassination was stoked anew in 1991, when Oscar-winning filmmaker Oliver Stone decided to make a movie about it. *JFK* is a star-studded, three-hour epic with a serious agenda. Almost three decades after the event, Stone's film introduced a new generation to magic bullets, secret plots, and shady government operatives. Critics praised the movie as "tremendously exciting," [110] but many also acknowledged how loose it played with the known facts.

What was especially disconcerting to some at the time of the film's release was the seamless way in which Stone blended actual news footage and dramatized scenarios with actors. Those unfamiliar with the real events—and even some who were—confessed they were often confused and wondered what was accurate and what was not.

At *JFK*'s center is former New Orleans district attorney Jim Garrison, a controversial figure in assassination circles. In Stone's movie, Garrison is portrayed as a hero—the first and only person to bring a prosecution in the murder. As played by Kevin Costner, Garrison is selfless, determined, and honorable. In real life, disagreement about Garrison's methods and ethics is plentiful.

In 1967 Garrison brought charges in the death of President Kennedy against a New Orleans businessman named Clay Shaw. While Shaw's motives were unclear in Garrison's indictment, the trial that ensued received wide coverage in the press. Garrison knew how to work the media and wove a dark and dangerous story involving Lee Harvey Oswald, Shaw, and a bizarre cast of characters. Oswald had spent time in New Orleans. Garrison claimed Oswald rented an office, that Shaw was fervently anti-Castro, and that his informant, Perry Raymond Russo, had witnessed a meeting between Shaw and Oswald. Also there, said

Garrison, was a creepy-looking fellow named David Ferrie.

At the meeting, reportedly held at a New Orleans party, Kurtz writes that Ferrie "launched into a verbal tirade against the Kennedy administration and voiced his intense desire to see President Kennedy, whom he labeled a communist, killed."[111] While Russo's account of the secret meeting compelled the presiding judge to order the arrest of Shaw, the rest of the investigation and eventual trial did not go as smoothly.

Ferrie was found dead in his apartment the day authorities were to serve him with an arrest warrant. Because of delays the trial did not begin until 1969. Under cross-examination, Russo, the main witness, was less than certain about what he saw at the party. Other witnesses were even less reliable. Kurtz says the real Garrison "smeared Shaw's good name and forced Shaw to spend a fortune in legal fees to defend himself against the fundamentally baseless charges."[112]

In the end, Stone made an intriguing movie that once again brought important questions about the assassination into focus. But historians also charge Stone with misrepresenting the known facts of the assassination. Stone admitted as much on the ABC News program *Nightline*: "Jim Garrison is a metaphor," he said. "I tried to put all the researchers from the 60's, and 70's, and the 80's into Jim's case. I took that liberty. That's dramatic license."[113]

E. Howard Hunt: The Last Word?

For spymaster E. Howard Hunt life was not a movie, although it might have appeared that way to outsiders—that is, if they had known what was going on next door. In 2004 the grand old man of the CIA was near death, suffering from a variety of ailments—

lupus, various cancers, and pneumonia. But he had one more secret to divulge before it was all over. In 2007 *Rolling Stone* magazine published a story about Hunt, a man who had been jailed over the Watergate scandal in the 1970s and was suspected of aiding in the execution of revolutionary Che Guevara in the 1960s.

Like Garrison, Hunt was a tough bird—stubborn and short-tempered. But Hunt, unlike the New Orleans D.A., lived a life of secrecy. At the CIA he traveled for months at a time, typically under an assumed name. He worked at the highest levels of the American government, but the specifics of his work were known to very few. Such is the life of a covert agent.

According to the *Rolling Stone* article, Hunt was a loyal soldier. "I had always assumed," he said, "that anything the White House wants was the law of the land."[114] In the world of covert intelligence, such loyalty implies a willingness to do things many would consider criminal, including murder.

On the surface, the Hunt family lived a typical suburban life, with a lovely house, a big yard, and a couple of cars in the driveway. Hunt's son, Saint John, knew very little about the dark side of his father's life while growing up. Instead, he more often than not suffered Hunt's wrath. The relationship between them was strained, to say the least. "He was a mean-spirited person and an extremely cruel father," remembers Saint John. And he set a high standard at home. "For the superspy not to have a superson was the ultimate disappointment."[115]

In 1975, after years living apart, the younger Hunt had a revelation. "I was in a phone booth in Maryland somewhere," he says. "I saw a poster on a telephone pole about who killed JFK, and it had a picture of three tramps." Staring at the poster more closely, he thought he recognized one of the tramps as his father.

Did You Know?

Kennedy was the first president born in the twentieth century.

E. Howard Hunt, wearing sunglasses, was a high-level CIA opera-tive. On the day of Kennedy's murder three men were photographed on the grassy knoll. Many believed these men were CIA operatives in disguise. Hunt's son was convinced one of the men was his father and claims that on his deathbed his father insinuated that Johnson ordered the hit on Kennedy. The Warren Commission virtually ig-nored evidence of the three's possible involvement.

"There's nobody that has all those same facial features. People say it's not him. He's said it's not him. I'm his son, and I've got a gut feeling." [116]

The three tramps in question had been spotted near the grassy knoll on the day of Kennedy's murder. While the Warren Com-mission virtually ignored evidence of their possible involvement, some conspiracy theorists are convinced these tramps were CIA agents in disguise.

Thirty years later the gravely ill Hunt passed a slip of paper to his son. On it, the old man had written "LBJ"—Lyndon Baines Johnson. Up to that time, the elder Hunt had always denied knowledge of Kennedy's assassin; now, he was telling his son that Kennedy's vice president had ordered the murder. Stunned, Saint John wanted to know more, and over the next few weeks he got what he asked for. According to his father, a complex network of CIA agents and a Mafia assassin named Lucien Sarti carried out the plot. The shots they fired came from the grassy knoll. While Howard Hunt claimed no direct involvement, he was there.

As further proof, Saint John made an audio recording of his father in 2004. Although Howard Hunt makes no specific accusations on tape, he says that Johnson had an "almost maniacal urge to become president. He regarded JFK as an obstacle to achieving that."[117]

To this day, Saint John Hunt is convinced by his father's outlandish but not impossible story. However, political ambition, as Johnson clearly had, does not equal murder. Unless more evidence is brought to light to corroborate what Hunt says happened, his charges against Lyndon Johnson will remain little more than rumor—a shot in the dark that has yet to yield conclusive results.

The Kennedy Mystique

Recent but unproven revelations like Hunt's are no doubt intriguing. Simply put, they sell newspapers. The Kennedy assassination is the story that will never die; Kennedy himself lives on through it. Every year, thousands of visitors from around the world visit Kennedy's grave, still the most popular attraction at Arlington National Cemetery. Much like the flame that lights his final resting place, Kennedy's legend will not be easily extinguished.

Although he had been in office for only 1,000 days, Kennedy's death elevated his reputation and transformed an unfinished presidency into a glorious one, at least in the eyes of the public. In national polls, Americans typically rank Kennedy as one of the best presidents, yet few know what he did. He is particularly popular among those born long after his abbreviated presidency.

The record shows that Kennedy made slow but steady progress on civil rights. He initiated a war on poverty and founded the Peace Corps, a government service organization that still encourages young people to volunteer around the world to help those less fortunate. Kennedy also strongly supported the nation's space program, and in 1969—six years after his death—NASA landed a man on the moon a year earlier than he predicted. Perhaps most important, he avoided all-out nuclear war with the Soviets during the Cuban Missile Crisis of 1962.

Controversially, Kennedy began U.S. military involvement in Vietnam. Under the Johnson and Nixon administrations, that conflict grew. By the late 1960s it spun out of control, costing over 58,000 American lives and the lives of 3.8 million Vietnamese civilians and soldiers. The last American forces left Vietnam in 1975.

Closer to home, Kennedy's bitter enemy Fidel Castro would not go quietly. He has led Cuba into the new millennium, yet his country's ties with the Soviet Union waned with the downfall of communism there. Castro's power also declined as did his health. The Cuban president would not step down until February 2008, at which time his brother, Raul, would take his place.

In the end, Kennedy's presidency was a promise unfulfilled. "He was this young man, glamorous young man," said Nicholas Katzenbach, deputy attorney general in the Kennedy administration, "whom I think had the potential to be a really great president. He

Most Americans Believe in a Conspiracy

More than 40 years after the assassination, 68 percent of the American public thinks there was some type of government conspiracy surrounding the assassination of President Kennedy. In 1966 only 46 percent thought a conspiracy made sense, most likely due to the Warren Commission's 1964 report having not been thoroughly scrutinized.

WHEN	PERCENT SUSPECTING A PLOT	PERCENT SUSPECTING ONE MAN
SEPTEMBER 1966	46%	34%
FEBRUARY 1967	44%	35%
SEPTEMBER 1967	60%	24%
NOVEMBER 1983	80%	13%
DECEMBER 1991	73%	11%
NOVEMBER 2003	70%	22%
NOVEMBER 2007	68%	N/A

Source: ABCNews.com, "Legacy of Suspicion: Decades After, Few Accept the Official Explanation for JFK Assassination," Gary Langer, November 16, 2007. http://abcnews.go.com.

was shot down before he really had much chance to prove it."[118]

Like Katzenbach, the consensus among historians is that Kennedy's accomplishments were modest, primarily because he was

cut down before being able to complete many of his goals. Many wonder what might have happened had he lived. For that reason, Kennedy captures the imagination as few other American leaders have. "Kennedy was someone who gave the country hope," says Robert Dallek. "He's become a kind of mythological figure, an iconic figure."[119]

New books are published each year about the legacy and times of John Fitzgerald Kennedy. Especially popular are the photographic volumes, portraying his large and vibrant family playing football at their Hyannis Port retreat or sitting silently as 1960 election returns announce a Kennedy victory. The family—started by father Joseph P. and Rose Fitzgerald Kennedy—portrayed itself as larger than life. Yet this unique American dynasty also wanted to be seen as down-to-earth and so like other Americans—or the way Americans like to imagine themselves.

Much of the Kennedy mystique was, therefore, self-generated. Writer Carl Sferrazza Anthony tells of a "prized hi-fi set in the West Sitting Hall right outside the door to Jackie's dressing room"[120] in the White House. Between the president's and First Lady's rooms sat a record player. According to legend, Kennedy would often sit in this passageway listening to records. One of his favorites was the score from *Camelot*, a popular musical of the day about King Arthur, Guinevere his queen, and the magical kingdom in which they lived. Today, when the Kennedys' time in the White House is recalled, so too is *Camelot's* title song, which speaks of a place that rain barely touches and where happiness is never darkened by tragedy. In Camelot, the lyrics say, the fairy tale ending comes true.

Every four years, as a new slate of candidates shake hands, kiss babies, and vie for the highest office in the land, comparisons to Kennedy are commonplace. For Democrats and Republicans alike, it is considered a compliment to appear "Kennedy-esque." Such a label implies that a politician is polished, articulate, and hopeful. It is clear that Kennedy's legacy shines brighter than ever through American politics. "There he is, our JFK," writes historian Michael Kazin, "the upswept hair, the decisive gesture, the buoyant grin. He will always be glancing toward a future that never arrives." [121]

"In the Cold"

For all the doubt, suspicion, and anger directed toward the Warren Commission, the opening statement of its report remains undeniable. Kennedy's assassination, it reads, "was a cruel and shocking act of violence directed against a man, a family, a nation, and against all mankind."[122]

Maybe for this reason, Americans still find such a heinous act difficult to reconcile. "At a time of emotional rupture," says writer Robert Goldberg, "conspiracy theories offer purpose and meaning." [123]

Attorney Vincent Bugliosi agrees, adding Americans crave such purpose because of a "general mistrust of government and the desire to imbue Kennedy's death with deeper meaning than a random act of violence or a simple relish for intrigue."[124] For journalist Robert Thompson, "It's become the one last great American mystery."[125]

When asked to name suspects today, Americans have a hard time, but they are convinced of one thing: Oswald did not act alone. Even Robert Kennedy believed fervently in a conspiracy. In 1963 he took a close look at the Cuba connection and the possibility that the mob had plotted to murder his brother.

In a recent *Time* magazine commentary, David Talbot writes that Robert Kennedy eventually "concluded Oswald was a member of

That's Why the Agent Is a Tramp

Shortly after the Kennedy assassination, three tramps (homeless people) were arrested at a train yard adjacent to Dealey Plaza. Although Harold Doyle, John Forester Gedney, and Gus Abrams were released soon thereafter, suspicion continued to swirl. Were these men, in fact, CIA agents with a hand in the assassination? One photo taken that day was especially arousing. The conspiracy-minded often refer to the resemblance between Gus Abrams, the oldest tramp, and E. Howard

the shadowy operation that was seeking to overthrow Castro." Furthermore, in a "revealing phone conversation with Harry Ruiz-Williams, a trusted friend in the anti-Castro movement, Kennedy said bluntly 'One of your guys did it.' Though the CIA and FBI were already working strenuously to portray Oswald as a Communist agent, Bobby Kennedy rejected this view."[126]

One could argue that as attorney general, the younger Kennedy had more access to classified information than most, and

john F. kennedy was
awarded the Pulitzer
Prize in 1957 for
his book of history
Profiles in Courage.

Hunt. Hunt's son is convinced Abrams and Hunt are the same man.

In 1989 a journalist took a close look at the men's criminal records. Doyle was hard to track, having moved around for much of his life. He was finally located in Oregon. Gedney had changed his life. After his time on the streets, he had pulled himself together, ending up a municipal officer in Florida. As for Abrams, the most suspicious, a researcher found his sister. Abrams, she said, was dead. Sister and brother had lived together for 15 years. She also recalled seeing the pictures of the tramps after their arrest. She was certain that Abrams was her brother.

therefore his certainty in the matter must be taken very seriously. Then again, grief can blind even the most sharp-sighted of family members. Tragically, Robert Kennedy was gunned down at the Ambassador Hotel in Los Angeles in 1968 while seeking the Democratic presidential nomination. He never had the chance to fully explore his hunch that his brother's murder was not the act of only one man.

Historians can also argue that the one thing Robert Kennedy

lacked was perspective. "People want to believe that the world is not that random—that things are not that chaotic, that something larger, bigger, was at stake here," says Dallek. "Because I think it's very difficult for them to accept the idea that someone as inconsequential as Oswald could have killed someone as consequential as Kennedy." [127]

Surviving members of the Warren Commission also balk at the notion that anyone other than Oswald conspired to murder the president. "The best proof," says commission attorney William T. Coleman, is that "it is 40 years later and nobody's come up with any statement of anybody else who did it." [128]

By looking carefully at what happened that day, and in the years that followed, the final answer may yet become clear. Then again, the mystery surrounding the assassination of John F. Kennedy may only intensify.

What remains beyond question is how deeply the nation felt the blow of the young president's untimely death—and how it is still feeling it. This human tragedy forever changed the way Americans view their leaders. For so many, something important was forever broken on November 22, 1963. For them, the pain lingers.

Eric Jones will never forget that pain. He heard the news as a Chatham, New Jersey, seventh grader. Today, as an attorney for the U.S. government, Jones can still recall how "personalized" [129] it was for the father of the nation to die so violently and so suddenly.

It was even more personal to Secret Service agent Clint Hill, who began having nightmares shortly after the assassination. Agents protecting the president are trained to not only watch carefully but, when necessary, to place themselves between the president and the threat. On that chilly November morning, Hill arrived seconds too late.

Legendary TV reporter Mike Wallace interviewed Hill years after that fateful day and found the agent's memories were still very fresh. If only he had reached the limousine "five-tenths of a second faster, or maybe a second faster, I wouldn't be here today," said Hill.

> WALLACE: You mean you would have gotten there and you would have taken the shot.
> HILL: The third shot, yes, sir.
> WALLACE: And that would have been all right with you?
> HILL: That would have been fine with me. [130]

Wallace described Hill as a "tormented man," one who paid the personal cost of surviving the president of the United States. For Kennedy assistant Arthur M. Schlesinger Jr., Kennedy was neither myth nor icon. He was a mentor and a close personal friend. In his memoir *A Thousand Days*, Schlesinger wrote of his grief—a grief made bearable only by his ability to share it with others:

> On December 22, a month after his death, fire from the flame burning at his grave in Arlington was carried at dusk to the Lincoln Memorial. It was fiercely cold. Thousands stood, candles in their hands; then, as the flame spread among us, one candle lighting the next, the crowd gently moved away, the torches flaring and flickering, into the darkness. The next day it snowed—almost as deep a snow as the inaugural blizzard. I went to the White House. It was lovely, ghostly and strange. It all ended, as it began, in the cold. [131]

"It is 40 years later and nobody's come up with any statement of anybody else who did it."

— Warren Commission attorney William T. Coleman, still waiting for a better answer.

NOTES

Introduction: "Death in the Family"
1. Eric Jones, interview by author, July 9, 2007.
2. Jones, interview.

Chapter 1: "Why Worry About It?"
3. Quoted in Newseum, with Cathy Trost and Sus Bennett, *President Kennedy Has Been Shot.* Naperville, IL: Sourcebooks, 2003, p. 14.
4. Quoted in Newseum, Trost, and Bennett, *President Kennedy Has Been Shot,* p. 4.
5. Quoted in Carl Sferrazza Anthony, *The Kennedy White House: Family Life and Pictures, 1961–1963.*New York: Simon & Schuster, 2001, p. 265.
6. Quoted in Robert Dallek, *An Unfinished Life.* London: Little, Brown, 2003, p. 693.
7. Quoted in ABC News, "The Kennedy Assassination: Beyond Conspiracy," *Peter Jennings Reports,* 2003.
8. Quoted in Charles Kenney, *John F. Kennedy.* New York: Public Affairs, 2000, p. 220.
9. Nellie Connally, with Mickey Herskowitz, *From Love Field: Our Final Hours with President John F. Kennedy.* New York: Rugged Land, 2003, p. 85.
10. Quoted in Newseum, Trost, and Bennett, *President Kennedy Has Been Shot,* p. 15.
11. Quoted in Newseum, Trost, and Bennett, *President Kennedy Has Been Shot,* p. 18.
12. Quoted in Newseum, Trost, and Bennett, *President Kennedy Has Been Shot,* p. 13.
13. Connally, with Herskowitz, *From Love Field,* p. 145.

14. Quoted in Newseum, Trost, and Bennett, *President Kennedy Has Been Shot,* p. 19.
15. Quoted in Newseum, Trost, and Bennett, *President Kennedy Has Been Shot,* p. 21.
16. Connally, with Herskowitz, *From Love Field,* p. 145.
17. Quoted in Connally, with Herskowitz, *From Love Field,* p. 146.
18. Quoted in PBS, "Who Was Lee Harvey Oswald?" *Frontline,* 2003. www.pbs.org.
19. Quoted in Kenney, *John F. Kennedy,* p. 223.
20. Quoted in Robert B. Semple Jr., ed., *Four Days in November.* New York: St. Martin's, 2003, p. 34.
21. Quoted in Semple, *Four Days in November,* p. 28.
22. Quoted in Semple, *Four Days in November,* p. 28.
23. Quoted in Newseum, Trost, and Bennett, *President Kennedy Has Been Shot,* p. 85.
25. Quoted in Semple, *Four Days in November,* p. 29.
26. Quoted in Newseum, Trost, and Bennett, *President Kennedy Has Been Shot,* p. 117.
27. Quoted in Newseum, Trost, and Bennett, *President Kennedy Has Been Shot,* p. 121.
28. Quoted in NBC News/PBS, *JFK Assassination: As It Happened,* 2008.
29. Quoted in NBC News/PBS, *JFK Assassination.*
30. Quoted in NBC News/PBS, *JFK Assassination.*

Chapter 2: Hunt for a Killer
31. Quoted in Semple, *Four Days in November,* p. 31.
32. Quoted in Semple, *Four Days in November,* p. 38.
33. Quoted in Gerald Posner, *Case Closed: Lee Harvey Oswald and the Assassination of JFK.* New

York: Random House, 1993, p. 4.

34. Quoted in Posner, *Case Closed*, p. 4.
35. Quoted in Posner, *Case Closed*, p. 5.
36. Quoted in PBS, "Who Was Lee Harvey Oswald?"
37. Quoted in Michael L. Kurtz, *The JFK Assassination Debates*. Lawrence: University Press of Kansas, 2006, p. 74.
38. Quoted in PBS, "Who Was Lee Harvey Oswald?"
39. Quoted in PBS, "Who Was Lee Harvey Oswald?"
40. Quoted in PBS, "Who Was Lee Harvey Oswald?"
41. Quoted in ABC News, "The Kennedy Assassination."
42. Quoted in PBS, "Who Was Lee Harvey Oswald?"
43. Quoted in Thomas Mallon, "Marina and Ruth," *New Yorker*, 2001, p. 5.
44. Quoted in Mallon, "Marina and Ruth," p. 9.
45. Quoted in Posner, *Case Closed*, p. 224.
46. Quoted in Posner, *Case Closed*, p. 224.
47. Quoted in PBS, "Who Was Lee Harvey Oswald?"
48. Quoted in PBS, "Who Was Lee Harvey Oswald?"
49. Quoted in Semple, *Four Days in November*, p. 455.
50. Quoted in Semple, *Four Days in November*, p. 466.
51. Quoted in Semple, *Four Days in November*, p. 467.

Chapter 3: Tangled Web: Calls of Conspiracy

52. Quoted in ABC News, "The Kennedy Assassination."
53. Quoted in ABC News, "The Kennedy Assassination."
54. Quoted in ABC News, "The Kennedy Assassination."
55. Henry Hurt, *Reasonable Doubt: An Investigation into the Assassination of John F. Kennedy*. Austin, TX: Holt, Rinehart & Winston, 1985, p. 61.
56. Hurt, *Reasonable Doubt*, p. 61.
57. Quoted in Hurt, *Reasonable Doubt*, p. 63.
58. Quoted in Kurtz, *The JFK Assassination Debates*, p. 86.
59. Kurtz, *The JFK Assassination Debates*, p. 127.
60. Quoted in Kurtz, *The JFK Assassination Debates*, p. 129.
61. Quoted in Kurtz, *The JFK Assassination Debates*, p. 129.
62. Quoted in Hurt, *Reasonable Doubt*, p. 110.
63. Quoted in Hurt, *Reasonable Doubt*, p. 111.
64. John Newman, *Oswald and the CIA*. New York: Carroll & Graf, 1995, p. xv.
65. Quoted in Newman, *Oswald and the CIA*, p. xvi.
66. Quoted in Newman, *Oswald and the CIA*, p. xvii.
67. Kurtz, *The JFK Assassination Debates*, p. 169.
68. Kurtz, The *JFK Assassination Debates*, p. 191.
69. Quoted in PBS, "Who Was Lee Harvey Oswald?"
70. Quoted in Dallek, *An Unfinished Life*, p. 359.
71. Quoted in Dallek, *An Unfinished Life*, p. 360.
72. Quoted in Dallek, *An Unfinished Life*, p. 363.
73. Dallek, An *Unfinished Life*, p. 365.
74. Quoted in ABC News, "The Kennedy Assassination."
75. Quoted in ABC News, "The Kennedy Assassination."
76. Quoted in ABC News, "The Kennedy Assassination."
77. Quoted in PBS, "Who Was Lee Harvey Oswald?"
78. Quoted in ABC News, "The Kennedy Assassination."
79. Quoted in ABC News, "The Kennedy Assassination."
80. Quoted in ABC News, "The Kennedy Assassination."
81. Quoted in Hurt, *Reasonable Doubt*, p. 170.

Chapter 4: Science and Suspicion

82. Quoted in PBS, "Who Was Lee Harvey Oswald?"
83. Quoted in PBS, "Who Was Lee Harvey Oswald?"
84. Quoted in PBS, "Who Was Lee Harvey Oswald?"
85. Quoted in ABC News, "The Kennedy Assassination."
86. Quoted in ABC News, "The Kennedy Assassination."
87. Quoted in ABC News, "The Kennedy Assassination."
88. Quoted in PBS, "Who Was Lee Harvey Oswald?"
89. Quoted in PBS, "Who Was Lee Harvey Oswald?"
90. Hurt, *Reasonable Doubt*, p. 74.
91. Quoted in ABC News, "The Kennedy Assassination."

92. Hurt, *Reasonable Doubt*, p. 76.
93. Quoted in ABC News, "The Kennedy Assassination."
94. Quoted in John Solomon, "Scientists Cast Doubt on Kennedy Bullet Analysis," *Washington Post*, May 17, 2007. www.washingtonpost.com.
95. Quoted in *Science Daily*, "Bullet Evidence Challenges Finding in JFK Assassination," May 17, 2007. www.sciencedaily.com.
96. Quoted in ABC News, "The Kennedy Assassination."
97. Quoted in ABC News, "The Kennedy Assassination."
98. Quoted in ABC News, "The Kennedy Assassination."
99. Quoted in PBS, "Who Was Lee Harvey Oswald?"
100. James H. Fetzer, "JFK Assassination Film Hoax: The Fast-Forward Mistakes," Assassination Science, March 22, 2007. www.assassination-science.com.
101. James H. Fetzer, "Posner's Selective Use of Evidence," Assassination Science, March 22, 2007. www.assassinationscience.com.
102. Quoted in *International Journal of the Humanities*, "Reasoning About Assassination," vol. 3, 2006.
103. Paul J. Hart, interview with author, July 25, 2007.
104. Hart, interview.
105. Hart, interview.
106. Quoted in Posner, *Case Closed*, p. 325.
107. Hart, interview.
108. Hart, interview.

Chapter 5: Case Closed . . . or Is It?

109. Kurtz, *The JFK Assassination Debates*, p. 223.
110. Quoted in Peter Travers, *JFK*, movie review, *Rolling Stone*, 1991. www.rollingstone.com.
111. Kurtz, *The JFK Assassination Debates*, p. 131.
112. Kurtz, *The JFK Assassination Debates*, p. 133.
113. Quoted in ABC News, "The Kennedy Assassination."
114. Quoted in Erik Hedegaard, "The Last Confessions of E. Howard Hunt," *Rolling Stone*, March 21, 2007. www.rollingstone.com.
115. Quoted in Hedegaard, "The Last Confessions of E. Howard Hunt."
116. Quoted in Hedegaard, "The Last Confessions of E. Howard Hunt."
117. Quoted in Saint John Hunt, "E. Howard Hunt: Testament," January 2004. www.saintjohn-hunt.com.
118. Quoted in ABC News, "The Kennedy Assassination."
119. Quoted in ABC News, "The Kennedy Assassination."
120. Anthony, *The Kennedy White House*, p. 67.
121. Quoted in Alan Brinkley and Davis Dyer, ed., *The American Presidency*. Boston: Houghton Mifflin, 2004, p. 408.
122. Warren Commission, *The Warren Commission Report*, ch.1, National Archives. www.archives.gov.
123. Quoted in ABC News, "The Kennedy Assassination."
124. Vincent Bugliosi, "The Assassination: Was It a Conspiracy? No," *Time*, July 2, 2007, p. 67.
125. Quoted in PBS, "Conspiracy Theories," *The NewsHour with Jim Lehrer*, November 20, 2003. www.pbs.org.
126. Quoted in David Talbot, "The Assassination: Was It a Conspiracy? Yes," *Time*, July 2, 2007, p. 66.
127. Quoted in ABC News, "The Kennedy Assassination."
128. Quoted in ABC News, "The Kennedy Assassination."
129. Jones, interview.
130. Quoted in NPR, "Mike Wallace, Interviewer: 'You and Me,'" *Fresh Air*, 2005. www.npr.org.
131. Arthur M. Schlesinger Jr., *A Thousand Days*. Boston: Houghton Mifflin, 1965, p. 1,031.

For Further Research

Books

Carl Sferrazza Anthony, *The Kennedy White House: Family Life and Pictures, 1961–1963.* New York: Simon & Schuster, 2001. An appropriate starting place for a fuller portrait of the Kennedy White House years. Anthony includes intimate family pictures alongside more official ones. The text is warm and inviting.

Robert Dallek, *An Unfinished Life.* New York: Little, Brown, 2003. Perhaps the best one-volume biography of the nation's thirty-fifth president. Dallek provides an excellent and detailed account of a singular life. He focuses in particular on Kennedy's many physical ailments, most of which were unknown to the general public at the time.

Charles Kenney, *John F. Kennedy.* New York: Public Affairs, 2000. Another interesting glimpse into the Camelot years. What sets this work apart is the archives culled from the John F. Kennedy Library in Boston. Included are excerpts of letters and government documents, some written in Kennedy's own hand.

Michael L. Kurtz, *The JFK Assassination Debates.* Lawrence University Press of Kansas, 2006. A respected skeptic attempts an objective look into the complex world of the Kennedy assassination. One helpful device is Kurtz's use of common questions related to the assassination and his thorough and well-researched responses.

Newseum, with Cathy Trost and Susan Bennett, *President Kennedy Has Been Shot.* Naperville, IL: Sourcebooks, 2003. A moment-by-moment account of what happened on the tragic ride through Dallas and in the hours immediately afterward. The book includes an audio CD containing radio news reports from that day.

New York Times Editors, *The Kennedy Years.* New York: Viking, 1964. A large, coffee-table volume with glorious and well-chosen black-and-white photographs of the Kennedy presidency. Articles by the *New York Times* staff offer a solid overview of the man and his times.

Robert B. Semple Jr., ed., *Four Days in November.* New York: St. Martin's, 2003. A fascinating look into the past, this volume reproduces the newspapers' accounts of those four terrible and confusing days. By reading each of the day's entries, researchers and students alike can peer into a veritable time capsule and piece together the information as it came in.

Web Sites

Assassination Science (www.assassinationscience. com). Leading conspiracy proponent James H. Fetzer's site is chock-full of new and evolving theories on who killed JFK and why.

John F. Kennedy Assassination Information Site (www.mcadams.posc.mu.edu). This is a fine site to start with because it provides an extensive overview of both the assassination and the myriad theories behind it.

John F. Kennedy Presidential Library and Museum (www.jfklibrary.org). Kennedy's true legacy was forged during his life. The JFK Library in Boston is one of the best resources for exploring the times and the policies of the nation's thirty-fifth president. The site also contains first-rate material for teachers of American history.

Who Was Lee Harvey Oswald? (www.pbs.org/ wgbh/pages/frontline/shows/oswald). PBS's award-winning *Frontline* produced a three-hour program on Oswald. This is the companion site. It has transcripts, photos, and links to other assassination-related Web sites.

INDEX

R

racism, 10
radio recording, 68
Randle, Linnie Mae, 33, 34
Reasonable Doubt (Hurt), 65
Rockefeller Commission, 64
Rolling Stone (magazine), 77
Roosevelt, Theodore, 8
Rubenstein, Jack "Ruby," 36 (illus), 37, 50, 58–59
Ruiz-Williams, Harry, 84
Russo, Perry Raymond, 75, 76

S

Schlesinger, Arthur M., Jr., 87
Secret Service
    entry/exit issue of fatal bullet and, 48
    motorcade route and, 14
    unidentified agent, 50
See also Hill, Clint
Seward, William, 45
Shaw, Clay, 75, 76
Shaw, Robert, 64–65
Shires, Tom, 22
Sidney, Hugh, 15
Silverman, Hillel, 59
Smith, Joe Marshall, 50
Smith, Merriman, 23
Southern states, 9–11
Soviet Union
    Cuba and, 45, 56, 80
    negotiations with, 9
    Oswald defection to, 32–33
    possible involvement in assassination, 45, 58
    relations with U.S., 44–45
space program, 80
Specter, Arlen, 63
Spiegelman, Cliff, 67
St. Matthew's Cathedral, 40
Stevenson, Adlai, 11
Stone, Oliver, 75, 76
Sturdivan, Larry, 66

T

Tague, James, 72–73
Talbot, David, 83–84

television
    assassination of Kennedy announced on, 19–20
    effect of, 8
    funeral on, 39–40
Texas
    popularity of Kennedy in, 9, 11
    reason for Kennedy trip to, 10
Texas School Book Depository, 27 (illus)
    bullets fired from, 26
    Oswald job at, 33–34
    spent cartridges in, 47
    two men seen in, 61
    witnesses placing Oswald in, 34–35
Texas Theatre, 28, 30 (illus)
Thomas, Evan, 45
Thompson, Robert, 83
Thousand Days, A (Schlesinger), 87
Time (magazine), 83–84
Times of London (newspaper), 38
Tippit, J.D., 7, 28–30
tracheotomy, 22, 55
Trade Mart, 14, 15, 18
tramps, 77–78, 84–85
Truly, Roy, 34

U

U.S. Marine Corps, 32

V

Valenti, Jack, 45
Vietnam, 80

W

Walker, C.T., 29
Walker, Edwin, 41
Wallace, Mike, 87
Warren, Earl, 45
Warren Commission
    ballistics tests, 65
    conclusions of, 46
    criticisms of
        changes in report, 47
        Magic Bullet I theory and, 46–47
        manipulated evidence to fit desired result, 48, 73

Oswald in Mexico City and, 51–52
    testimony of eyewitnesses and, 49–50
    goals of, 44, 45
    members, 45, 45 (illus), 47, 63, 86
    public opinion about, 74
    weapons
    for attempted assassination of Walker, 41
    markings on bullets and, 66
    ownership of, 45
    package in Frazier car, 34
    size of wound and, 64–65
    Williams, Bonnie Ray, 34
witnesses
    account of Zapruder, 17
    to bullets fired from grassy knoll, 26–27, 50
    number of shots heard by, 61–62
    placing Oswald in Book Depository, 34–35
    to Ruby and Oswald on grassy knoll, 49–50
    to shots from Book Depository, 26
    to shots from railroad tower, 27
    to Tippit murder, 28
    to two men seen in Book Depository, 61
    to unidentified Secret Service agent, 50
wounds
    entrance/exit issue, 22, 48, 49, 54–55, 67
    location of fatal wound, 49
    size of, 64–65
    sustained by Connally, 73
    sustained by Tague, 72–73
    in Zapruder film, 70

Z

Zapruder, Abraham
    eyewitness account of, 17
    film by
        camera used, 7, 8
        computer analysis of, 62–64
        as fake, 69–70
        Kennedy's movements on, 67
        length of, 8
        sale of, 7

ABOUT THE AUTHOR

David Robson is a playwright, freelance writer, and English professor. His plays have been performed from Florida to Alaska. He is the recipient of a National Endowment for the Arts grant and two fellowships from the Delaware Division of the Arts. David's interest in the Kennedy assassination began when he was a child with the photographic book *The Kennedy Years*, published in 1964. The book now sits on his bookshelf in Wilmington, Delaware, where he lives with his wife and daughter.